Maternity care

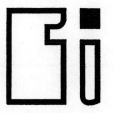

Tilburg Studies on Health Care

1

Edited by the

Institute for Health Care Research

of the Tilburg School of Economics, Social Sciences and Law

A Study on Public Health

Maternity care
A socio-economic analysis

R. M. Lapré
Secretary Planning Department
of the Central Council for Public Health, The Hague

Foreword by
J. B. Stolte,
Professor of Hospital Sciences,
Tilburg School of Economics, Social Sciences and Law and
the University of Nijmegen

1973
Tilburg University Press
The Netherlands

Tilburg University Press

is the result of concurring ideas of the Tilburg Institute of Economics and the publishing-houses Rotterdam University Press and Wolters-Noordhoff Publishing, Groningen, the Netherlands.

ISBN 90 237 2911 0

Distributors: Academic Book Services Holland, P.O. Box 66, Groningen, the Netherlands

Translated by Margeret van den Bergh-Marshall, Vught, Holland.

To my parents

Foreword

Everywhere nowadays there is disquietude about the development of the health service as part of the social system. On the one hand a great deal, too much perhaps, is expected and demanded of it. On the other hand there is serious concern about continually increasing costs, the more so because there seems to be no way of keeping them in check. The individual consumer and those whose collective demands are dealt with by compulsory and private insurance companies feel themselves to be dependent on the arbitrary decisions of the monopolists – members of the medical profession and the institutions. Moreover, it happens with increasing frequency that there is not sufficient manpower available to supply the services demanded. Neither the consumer nor the producer is in a position to bring hard facts to bear upon the problem so the discussion remains vague and unconvincing. There are, therefore, fairly good grounds for suggesting that health services should be provided in an arrangement whereby acceptable results are achieved at the lowest cost. However, this will still have to be proved on the evidence of hard facts and these are mostly lacking. Dr. Lapré's study is one of the very few attempts to supply them. It is sincerely to be hoped that others will follow his example.

J. B. Stolte

Preface

This publication is, for the most part, taken from the thesis on which, in 1972, I was awarded a Doctor's degree in Economics at the University of Tilburg. It is based on the work that I carried out as scientific assistant in the Department of Hospital Sciences and Public Health. This research was made possible by a subsidy provided by the Praeventiefonds in The Hague.

Since its appearance in Dutch, there have been many suggestions that I should make my study of maternity care in the Netherlands available to readers outside this country through a translation into English. I was, therefore, pleased to know that the University Press Rotterdam/Tilburg and the publishing firm of Wolters-Noordhoff were contemplating such an edition.

In the writing of my thesis I received the help and support of a great many people, two of whom I must mention separately as being particularly deserving of my gratitude. Dr. J. B. Stolte, Professor of Hospital Sciences and Public Health at the Universities of Tilburg and Nijmegen made a substantial contribution to my work on which his advice and stimulating influence have, I feel, clearly impressed their mark. Naturally, I am personally responsible for any shortcomings that might appear. The second person is my wife, without whose encouragement the thesis would probably never have been written. Not only did she help me wherever possible but she ensured for me a most pleasant atmosphere in which to work by her gift of making the most of 'ups' and dispelling the 'downs'.

I consider myself fortunate in having found M. v. d. Bergh-Marshall willing to undertake the translation of my study and I hope that this English version will stimulate a wider interest in maternity care in the Netherlands.

Contents

XI

1. The research

Changes are continually taking place in the system adopted for supplying the public with any particular part of the health service. The reason is to be found in new and different social conditions as well as in the development of medical knowledge and ability. Maternity care in the Netherlands is, fortunately, very different to-day from that provided 50 years ago and the results of the present system may justifiably be considered as a triumph and a blessing. Gone are the days when high rates of ante-natal, perinatal and maternal mortality were regarded as typical and inherent risks of childbirth.

The maternity services now available in the Netherlands are proving themselves to be most satisfactory and have earned for this country a high place on the international ladder of success according to the generally accepted standards.

Perinatal mortality – by which is meant the number of infants that die before birth and after the 28th week of pregnancy, plus the new-born babies that die in the first week after birth, per 1000 live and still-births, is amongst the lowest in the world. (Verbrugge 1968, Haire 1971). Death of mothers in childbirth is also very low. (Bout 1971). By international comparison, the Dutch record appears even more favourable if the average age of the patients is taken into account.

However, there are countries where perinatal and maternal mortality are still lower than they are here. These countries have a system of maternity care that differs from that of the Netherlands in that practically all deliveries take place in hospital. It is a notable fact that in this country, both confinement and post-natal care take place in the home unless there are reasons why this should not be the case. This fact forms the basis of the Dutch system. It is, however, a basis which for some years, has been and continues to be, a subject for increasing discussion.

1

For various reasons, there is a growing tendency for confinements to take place in hospital but there is no unanimous opinion as to the value of this development.

The trend towards increasing hospitalization which has been in progress for some years now, involves important financial and organizational questions. The scarcity of qualified experts in the field of maternity care such as general practitioners, specialists, midwives, nurses and maternity aids, gives special significance to reflections on the efficacy of the present pattern of consumption.

In any enquiry into the use made of maternity services, the consumer must not be disregarded.

What are the consumers' wishes? How did the demand for maternity services arise and what value do the consumers and their associates attach to the services provided for them?.

In references to maternity care we include not only natal but also ante-natal and post-natal care. Ante-natal care is that which takes place during pregnancy, natal care at the time of actual delivery, and post-natal care up to about 10 days after delivery.

In the framework of maternity care, services are demanded and offered. There may be said to be a 'market' for maternity services. In the course of this study, an attempt has been made to gain some insight into this market. The following are some of the questions that were considered: 'What kind of services are negotiated and to what extent? What is the market behaviour of consumers and suppliers and how can this be explained?

How can the market be characterized with regard to the number of participants, the transparency of the market and the nature of the services provided? To what extent does the Government exercise control over this market? What prices are asked for the various services and how were they determined?'

2. METHOD AND MATERIAL USED FOR ENQUIRY

Our data was obtained from literature, from interviews with 400 women and from material furnished by the Council for Medical Registration (Stichting Medische Registratie) in Utrecht concerning a very large number of hospital deliveries.

2

a. *Field research*
The facts obtained from literature were not thought to be sufficient to provide an answer to the questions put forward in the introduction. It was considered important to supplement this data with the experiences, opinions and wishes of a number of women who had had experience of maternity services. For this purpose, a field enquiry was set up whose aspects were chiefly of an exploratory nature. This type of enquiry seeks to bring about a widening of the basis of knowledge. In it, we are not yet concerned with representativity.

In view of considerable differences in the demand for maternity services between small and large districts, research areas were sought where the differences would be clearly demonstrated. For that reason, districts were chosen where, in the year 1967, the distribution of domiciliary and institutional confinements was the same as that of the country as a whole. Of the smaller districts, those were selected with a population of less than 5,000 inhabitants. The large districts have a population of more than 100,000 inhabitants, but fewer than 500,000. For practical reasons, the enquiry was limited to districts in the provinces of Utrecht and North Brabant. In each of these provinces, one large and three small neighbouring districts were selected. A total of 400 women were interviewed (not counting the test interviews). The distribution of the 400 interviews amongst the districts covered by the enquiry was as follows: 100 in the district of Utrecht and 100 in the combined districts of Linschoten, Benschop and Snelrewaard; 100 in Tilburg and 100 in Haaren, Helvoirt and Alphen combined.

The interviews concerned married women who had been confined in the period 1st January 1970-30th June 1970 and whose infant had been entered as live-born in the population registers of the districts concerned. It was through these registers that the addresses of the women could be ascertained. The women interviewed in the districts of Tilburg and Utrecht were selected at random. As regards the rural districts that were examined, the following method was followed; in both the area around Utrecht and that around Tilburg, 2 districts were chosen of which the total population of women concerned in the enquiry were interviewed. In the third district, the women were selected at random until the required number of 100 respondents had been reached.

The interviews took place in the months of September, October and November 1970. They were carried out by a small group of specially instructed female interviewers whose proposed visit was made known

3

beforehand by letter which also contained further information about the purpose of the enquiry. There was no lack of willingness to take part in the enquiry and most of the women seemed to welcome the opportunity to discuss their confinement. Only a very small number of the interviews proved to be 'hard-going' in this respect. On an average, the interviews lasted an hour and a half. There were 16 re-fusals to co-operate: 10 in Utrecht, 3 in Tilburg, 2 in the area around Utrecht and 1 in the area around Tilburg.

Moreover, a number had to be discounted as a result of house-moving (19), continual absence (7), and incorrect addresses (4). There were, however, sufficient addresses in reserve to make good these losses and to maintain the desired number of 400 interviews. A provisional questionnaire was tested on 20 respondents and this was followed by a final version which comprised both pre-coded and so-called open-end questions. It also included a number of statements, partly for use as check questions and partly to provide extra information.

The respondents concerned in the field research.[1]
Of the 400 respondents, 25 % came from the district of Utrecht and 25 % from the district of Tilburg. 25 % of them were divided amongst the rural districts round Utrecht in the following proportions: Lin-schoten 13 %, Benschop 10 % and Snelrewaard 3 %. The districts round Tilburg provided another 25 % as follows: Alphen 11 %, Haaren 10 % and Helvoirt 4 %.

Since half the respondents were living in a predominantly Catholic region and the other half in a mixed area, it is not surprising that the total group investigated included a strikingly large number of Roman Catholics, viz. 67 %. 15 % were Dutch Reformed Church and 11 % had no religion. For the country as a whole these percentages were, in the year 1960: 40 %, 29 % and 18 % respectively (according to Central Office of Statistics 1971).

Most of the respondents belonged to the 25/29 age-group (38 %) followed by the 20/24 year group (30 %) and the 30/34 year group (19 %). Considerably smaller percentages were found in the other age-groups. (For the country as a whole in 1969 the percentages were 34 %, 33 % and 18 % respectively).

Classification of the group according to level of education was carried out in accordance with standards applied by the Central Office of

1. Percentages adjusted to round figures.

4

Statistics (1968). The levels of education attained by the respondents were as follows: basic and primary education 30.5 %, further primary education 55 %, secondary education 10 %, intermediate and higher education 4 %. (For the country as a whole and with reference to the population of working women, the percentages in 1960 were 54 %, 37 %, 8 % and 1% respectively).

The respondents had children according to the following percentages: 1 child 36 %, 2 children 38 %, 3 children 14 %, 4 or more children 12 %. (In 1960, for the country as a whole and referring to married couples with children living at home, the wife being younger than 45 years old, the figures were as follows: 1 child 27 %, 2 children 32 %, 3 children 19 %, 4 or more children 22 %).

The respondents were classified in 'social levels' according to the occupation of their husbands. The criterium applied for this purpose was that of van Tulder (1962) which is based on an assumption of 6 social levels whereby the lowest number in the scale refers to the highest level and the highest number to the lowest level. 13 % of the respondents belonged to the social levels I and II, 45 % to the levels III and IV, whilst 41% belonged to the 'lower' social levels.

64 % of the respondents were covered by the compulsory health insurance scheme, (51% for the country as a whole) 13 % by a voluntary health insurance scheme (13 % for the country as a whole) and 19 % were privately insured. 3 % were covered by other insurances (including those for Government employees). One respondent was not insured.

Employees in the Netherlands whose income is below a fixed minimum (18.800 guilders per year in 1971) automatically fall under the compulsory health insurance scheme (Ziekenfonds). Self-employed persons and others with an income below the fixed minimum may, if they wish, become voluntary members of the ziekenfonds. In this publication, whenever reference is made simply to 'ziekenfonds insured', this includes both the compulsorily and the voluntarily insured. Privately insured people have an income above the fixed minimum and are excluded from participation in the ziekenfonds.

Income is an important factor in deciding how to insure against the expenses of illness. In general people with a net monthly income of less than ± 1050 guilders were insured under the compulsory health insurance scheme. 15 % of the respondents had a net monthly income lower than 650 guilders, 37 % of them had an income of 650 to 850 guilders, whilst 20 % had an income of 850 to 1050 guilders. In all, 72 % had an income of 1050 guilders and less). 10 % belonged to the

5

income group of 1050 to 1250 guilders, whilst 9 % had 1250 guilders or more. The income of 9 % of the women was not known. (For the country as a whole in 1967: taxpayers with children and an annual income of less than 10,000 guilders 36 %, between 10 and 15,000 guilders 36 %, between 15 and 20,000 guilders 12 %, 20,000 guilders and more 15 %).

b. *Information supplied by the Council for Medical Registration*
The information supplied by the Council for Medical Registration concerned hospital confinements. It included among other things, information about care and management during labour, length of stay, referral to hospital and the way in which patients were insured.

The hospitals affiliated to the Council send information regularly about their patients (who naturally remain anonymous) to the Central Office of Registration in Utrecht. There the information is processed and surveys are sent at regular intervals to the affiliated hospitals. Besides giving data relating to the particular hospital in question, these surveys also supply information gathered from all participating hospitals. The governing-body of the Council gave permission for reports to be made available on women who had been admitted to the affiliated hospitals for their confinements in the years 1966 to 1970. The reports dealt with a total of approximately 175,000 deliveries and the information they contained was computerized at the University of Tilburg.

There are upwards of 1 million admissions to Dutch hospitals every year, a large number of them being to institutions affiliated to the Council for Medical Registration. The following list shows the percentages of admissions registered by the Council in the years covered by this enquiry.

1966	1967	1968	1969	1970
28	33	42	± 50	± 60

A great many deliveries were recorded by the Council and, as shown by the following figures, the numbers increased considerably with each successive year.

1966	1967	1968	1969	1970
17,113	24,380	34,545	46,142	53,938

The total number of hospital deliveries was as follows: (source of information CSB/GHI)

6

1966	1967	1968	1969	1970
74,445	78,950	82,327	91,824	91,914

Thus, in 1966, about 1 in 4 hospital deliveries was registered by the Council and in 1970, this was the case with more than half of them.

The hospitals where deliveries take place can be sub-divided into general hospitals, teaching hospitals and special maternity hospitals. The total number of these institutions as compared with the number of those taking part in the central registration is as follows:

	National Total * 1970	Numbers taking part in registration 1970
General hospital	205	102
Teaching hospitals	9	6
Maternity hospitals	4	2
	218	110

* National Hospital Institute 1970.

From this it may be concluded that in 1970 half the hospitals were associated with the Council for Medical Registration and that the different categories were proportionately represented.

The number of hospitals taking part in registration related to their size was as follows:

	National Total	Numbers taking part in registration
Fewer than 125 beds		
125 to 249 beds	75	33
250 to 374 beds	55	38
375 to 499 beds	23	14
500 and more beds	31	18
	218	110

The smallest hospitals were least represented. In view of the relatively small part played by these hospitals in the total amount of service provided, not much importance need be attached to them.

7

2. General outline of services based on information from literature

1. THE SERVICES[1]

Antenatal care

A woman who is pregnant, or thinks she is, will generally consult a family doctor or a midwife about her condition. In fact, in order to have the pregnancy confirmed, she will go to the person who, in the normal course of events, will attend her delivery. After this preliminary examination, she will want supervision and regular antenatal care throughout the pregnancy. Sometimes, steps will have to be taken to ensure the best possible condition of both mother and child and often too, instruction and advice will be needed.

Since 1951, following an alteration to article 15 of the Law governing Medical Practice, midwives have been authorized to provide antenatal service in cases of 'normal' pregnancy. In other than normal cases they, the midwives, are required by law to consult a doctor or to refer the patient to a doctor.

The family doctor (general practitioner) is subjected to no such restrictions though, in the case of a woman at risk or in the event of extensive diagnostical apparatus being required, he will normally pass his patient on to a hospital consultant.

A pregnancy is considered abnormal if there are deviations from the usual physiological pattern i.e. pathological cases. A pregnant woman is said to be at risk when her condition is such as to be considered a threat to her normal physiological development and that of her child.

The factors that give rise to an at risk situation can be grouped under the headings – biological, pathological and social (NIPG 1965). Biological factors include advanced age, and/or high parity of the mother, primiparae over the age of 30-35 years, grandes multiparae

1. See page 30 for sketch plan.

8

after the age of 35 years, multiple pregnancy, prematurity. Pathological factors include abnormal position (e.g. breach position), prejudicial obstetrical anamnesis, toxaemia, rhesus antagonism, obstetrical operations, anaemia. Social factors include illegitimacy, bad social-economic circumstances and insufficient facilities for the provision of medical attention.

The risk increases if there is more than one factor to be considered. One important aim of the antenatal services provided by family doctors and midwives is that of selecting women at risk. Partly because of the facilities and equipment at his disposal, the services of a specialist are considered more adequate in an at risk situation than those of a general practitioner or midwife.

In 1950, in order to assist general practitioners and midwives in their antenatal work, consultation clinics for antenatal care were initiated with the backing of a Government subsidy. However, family doctors and midwives made but limited use of the service and for this reason the clinics never really got off the ground.

In 1963 a team of doctors from the Dutch General Practitioners' Association, recognizing the importance of an early start to antenatal care, set up an enquiry to find out at what stage in their pregnancy women first reported to their family doctor. It was found that townswomen reported on an average 16 days earlier than countrywomen. Women from the higher social classes reported sooner than those from the lower ones. It was also found that, on an average, the more children the women already had, the longer they delayed their visit to the doctor.

The age of the woman did not much affect the decision as to when the first visit should be made. The enquiry carried out by Hennink in 1966 showed that it was particularly the women in the lower income groups who, on average, deferred their visit the longest.

Apart from the services provided in the antenatal period by family doctor, midwife or specialist, there are also those of the different Cross societies, such as gymnastic classes and talks on motherhood or parenthood. Expectant mothers who have booked a maternity nurse also receive instruction from the staff of the maternity centre.

Natal care
During confinement the maternity patient requires obstetric assistance which both doctors and midwives are qualified to give. In the case of midwives however, the qualification is valid only for straightforward deliveries. Doctors who attend confinements are almost always general practitioners or specialists (gynaecologist-obstetricians).

9

As a rule, both general practitioners and midwives attend the maternity patient in her own home, specialists almost always in a hospital. As a result, the specialist is in a position, if necessary, to call on the assistance of most highly-qualified experts. Adequate medical attention during confinement can be provided only where suitable accommodation is available and this is not always the case in the patient's own home. In that case, it may be decided to make use of accommodation provided by a maternity institution or hospital. The condition of the patient may necessitate the availability of particular apparatus (e.g. for performing operations) and of certain other precautionary measures such as, for instance, blood banks which, as a rule, are to be found only in a hospital.

The doctor or midwife in charge of the confinement needs assistance and this is given by (student) maternity helps and (student) nurses. The former help with domiciliary deliveries and the latter with hospital deliveries.

Post-natal care

In the post-natal period both mother and child need nursing and care. These are provided in the home by, for instance, maternity helps and also in hospital or maternity home by trained nurses.

When mother and child remain at home, there must be domestic help for the whole family. This may be undertaken by maternity helps, relations or other suitable persons. It is usual for the maternity help to stay with the family for 8 to 10 days after the delivery, from 8 o'clock in the morning till 6 or 7 o'clock in the evening in order to nurse, care for and keep under observation both mother and child, and also to take the mother's place with regard to housekeeping (internal maternity care). Some of the work of the 'internal' maternity help may also be delegated to the visiting maternity service. In that case, the maternity help calls once or twice a day for one or two hours, but only to nurse and care for mother and child. This means that less attention can be paid to observation and none to housekeeping.

When mother and child are away from home during the post-natal period, some arrangements have to be made for the rest of the family and this might mean that domestic help is required. In the meantime, mother and baby are provided with 'hotel service' in hospital or maternity institution and are, moreover, assured of the availability of all the other facilities with which those places are equipped.

10

Package services
The demand in respect of maternity services is for a 'package comprising a particular combination of antenatal, natal and postnatal care. The various services included in the package are complementary to each other; they supplement each other and conjointly fulfil the needs of the different patients.

The contents of the package of maternity services may vary with each individual. Among those frequently in demand are:

a. supervision by the family doctor during pregnancy, obstetric assistance by the family doctor, assistance of the maternity help at the delivery, domiciliary arrangements, nursing, care and domestic assistance to be given by the maternity help during the postnatal period.
b. the same as the foregoing but with antenatal care and assistance at delivery to be provided by the midwife.
c. antenatal care and obstetric assistance by a consultant, availability and use of hospital facilities, assistance of nursing staff during postnatal period, nursing assistance and care, hotel services and the availability of facilities.

Maternity services may be provided in the home, in hospital or in a maternity home.

According to the Health Department definition (GHI 1970), a hospital is an institution to which patients can be admitted under the terms of the compulsory insurance scheme with the exception of psychiatric institutions, sanatoria for tubercular patients, clinics for nervous complaints and most military hospitals. Deliveries take place in the general hospitals (205), in the teaching hospitals (9), and in the special maternity hospitals (4). In 1968, of all babies born in hospital 82% were born in a general hospital, 11% in a teaching hospital and 7% in a special maternity hospital. These latter are equipped with an operating theatre and a blood bank.

It should be observed that the total number of hospital births does not correspond with the total number of births that take place other than in the home (so-called intramural deliveries).

The total of intramural deliveries assessed by the Central Office for Statistics includes those that took place in maternity homes. These are equipped with operating theatres and blood banks. Concerning intramural deliveries, the Central Office for Statistics differentiates between general hospitals, teaching hospitals, schools of midwifery, recognized maternity homes, non-recognized maternity homes, non-recognized nursing homes, and other non-recognized institutions. The various kinds of non-recognized institutions are of minor importance (a total number of 1811 births in 1968). In the same year (1968) 8718 babies were born in the recognized maternity homes.

2. PARTICIPANTS IN THE MARKET

a. *The demand side of the market*
About 240,000 births take place in the Netherlands each year (CBS 1971) and the number of maternity packages demanded per year is roughly the same. Since 1961, with the exception of the year 1969, the number of births per 1000 women aged 15 to 44 years has been continually decreasing (from 117.8 in 1955/1964 to 99.1 in 1970).

For the Netherlands as a whole, one might say that there are 'many buyers' (polyopsony). However, in the framework of a concrete market which is generally to be found within a limited geographic area (neighbourhood, municipality, district) there is a situation of 'few buyers' (oligopsony).

The demand for maternity services is spread over the year. However, there are more births in Spring than in the rest of the year. In 1970 there were 18.3 live births per 1000 inhabitants while in the months March, April and May averaged over the rest of the year, there were 19.5.

Various factors can be indicated as influencing the choice of maternity services.

In the first place, there is the need for them on medical grounds. For instance, if a surgical operation is necessary, or in the event of continuous or specialized care being required, a domiciliary confinement is out of the question. (De Haas-Postuma 1962 and Verbrugge 1968 have carried out important studies on the subject of domiciliary confinements.)

The choice is also influenced by social circumstances such as living-conditions and family circumstances. Consumers are only to a limited extent in a position to judge what services they need. In particular, it is impossible for them to assess the need for medical help. Therefore the consumers cannot decide independently what services and facilities will be required in their own individual circumstances.

It is partly the heterogenity of the services offered that makes it difficult for the consumer to appraise their quality and it is largely the suppliers who determine the demand on the part of the consumers (e.g. by deciding that there are medical indications) or who at least influ-

12

ence the demand by their information and advice. If the suppliers advise medical necessity for particular services, the influence of price on demand is of small significance (low elasticity). There seems to be greater elasticity with regard to demand arising from social factors.

In another way, the demand is influenced by financial considerations. This is evident in the case of women who avail themselves of services provided free of charge although they would, in fact, prefer other services. Opinions as to the value of the various services, whether or not they are well-founded, are also contributory factors to the decision.

Of further significance is the possibility of choosing from various different service packages. For instance, the number of hospital deliveries will decrease to the extent that a) general practioners have sufficient time and skill to conduct domiciliary deliveries; b) that there are sufficient practising midwives and c) that there is an adequately-staffed organization to look after and nurse the maternity patient and her baby.

Lastly, geographical circumstances have to be considered, since people are more likely to make use of facilities that are near at hand than of those that are some distance away. A case in point is the difference in the use of hospital services by urban populations on the one hand and rural populations on the other. However, there are cases in which distance necessitates the use of certain services for precautionary reasons when the immediate availability of services is of importance.

An illustration of this is the admission to hospital of patients for whom because of distance, transfer to hospital in a short space of time would be impossible should medical problems arise during a domiciliary confinement. The conception of distance includes also situations where difficulty of access to the patient's domicile makes speedy and safe transfer to hospital impossible (e.g. flat-dwellings and apartments without lifts).

On the demand side of the market the compulsory and the private health insurance occupy a special place. They represent combined purchasing power (Stolte 1965) and they safeguard an important part of the demand for maternity services. Demand is stimulated by the fact that maternity services are included in insurance benefits. There are in the Netherlands almost 100 compulsory health insurance societies, upwards of 100 private ones and 14 for government and local government employees. Full re-imbursement is made, to women compulsorily insured, for the services of a midwife (including antenatal and postnatal care).

13

b. *The supply side of the market*
The supply side of the market is limited to the producers belonging to that particular 'branch of service'. This latter can be defined as: the aggregation of suppliers (persons and institutions) engaged in supplying the various kinds of services connected with maternity care. Between certain of these services there is a relatively high substitution-elasticity (e.g. between those of general practitioner, midwife and specialist as well as between facilities in the home, in hospital and in a maternity home). Alternatively, the services are complementary to each other (e.g. obstetric service, help during delivery, nursing/care and hotel services).

Although there are in the Netherlands (approximately) 4500 practising general practitioners, 775 midwives and 330 gynaecologists, and in spite of the fact that deliveries can be carried out in upwards of 200 hospitals and 20 recognized maternity homes, we still feel that, from the point of view of a concrete market, there are not 'many suppliers' (polypoly).
  The supply is spread over place and time.
The demand for and the supply of maternity services is substantive only within certain geographical areas which cannot be exactly defined. The demand for maternity services by a patient in Amsterdam is of no concern to a doctor in Maastricht because of the distance between the two. In the same way, offers of outpatient maternity service in a hospital in Alkmaar are hardly of interest to a patient in Utrecht. Within a particular geographical area there is generally a situation of 'few' market subjects (oligopoly).

General practitioner, midwife, specialist
Births related to 'supplier' of obstetric assistance (CBS 1971)

	1958	1963	1967	1968	1969
Medical practitioner	61.9	64.6	63.9	63.3	63.0
Midwife	38.1	35.5	36.0	36.5	36.8

As the above table shows the medical practitioners' share in the market was smaller in 1967 than in 1963 and continued to diminish in 1968 and 1969. On the other hand, the midwives' share increased in the same years though even so, it was less in 1969 than in 1958.

The withdrawal by many general practitioners from the market for obstetric services is an important factor in the drop in the percentage

14

of domiciliary deliveries. Of similar importance is the reduction in the number of midwives with an independent practice. There is a noticeable and increasing tendency among midwives to prefer employment with a hospital or maternity home. In the future, midwives employed by maternity centres of the Cross Societies will probably be supervising domiciliary deliveries. The question put to the Council for compulsory insurance by the then Secretary of State for Health and Social Affairs as to whether maternity assistance given to compulsorily insured patients could also be provided by institutions is pertinent in this connection. Evaluation of obstetric service in general practice can be found in publications by Pel and Pel-Mellink (1962), the Society of Dutch General practitioners (1962 and 1966), Hennink (1966) and Verboom (1968). These studies suggest that there are fairly big differences in the maternity side of general practice.

Publications concerning midwives include those issued by the Inspector of Public Health (1963, 1967, 1968 and 1969), and also studies by van der Sande (1966), van Elderen-van der Meer (1967), Verbrugge (1968) and Oostveen (1971). With regard to independent midwives, a picture presents itself of a group of professional women whose position, for various reasons, is being subjected to pressure. The main reason appears to be the fact that maternity work has developed in a way that makes it an integral part of medical care and this threatens the position of the independent midwife. There are other reasons, including increasing hospitalization especially in the big towns which provide the largest part of the midwives' share of the market, increased prosperity, ease of access to the family doctor, as well as the feeling that exists among some members of the public that a midwife is less adept than a doctor. It has been suggested that, in order to obtain better opportunities to carry out her practice, the midwife would be advised to join forces with a doctor and to seek engagement by a hospital or maternity home.

Organized maternity care
In 1964, general practitioners were assisted at about 80% of their domiciliary deliveries by maternity helps or student maternity helps employed by a maternity centre. In the case of deliveries performed by midwives, the percentage was 30. At about two thirds of the deliveries supervised by midwives there was no trained help present. This was the case in about 10% of the doctors' deliveries. (Verbrugge 1965) According to the records of the Inspector of Public Health (1971), the percentage of deliveries supervised in 1970 by a midwife without any

15

official maternity help was still 35. In respect of the doctors, the percentage remained at about 10. One explanation for the fact that family doctors and maternity helps work together more often than midwives and maternity helps is that there is a comparatively large amount of organized maternity care in rural areas which is where most of the doctors' deliveries take place. At various maternity centres where there was a shortage of maternity helps, it became customary to give priority to deliveries supervised by doctors.

With the exception of 1970, the number of cases of internal maternity help increased steadily at the cost of domiciliary confinements without official maternity care.

In absolute figures the number of confinements under the care of maternity centres that took place in the years 1966 to 1970 (GHI 1971) were as follows:

1966	120,103
1967	123,264
1968	124,591
1969	127,241
1970	121,539

As percentages of the number of births respectively 49.1; 50.4; 52.3; 51.1; 50.5.

Of all the maternity care offered in 1970, 78.4 % was provided in the form of internal care, 15 % in the form of visiting maternity care, while 6.4 % of the cases were a combination of types.

The nature of the care provided in districts of varying size was not uniform. The number of internal-care cases was relatively smaller and the number of cases of visiting maternity-care relatively larger in the larger districts. The rest – those without any organized maternity care were relatively few in the larger districts.

The proportions of each category differed considerably from province to province. Relatively low percentages of internal care were found in Groningen (61.4 %) and Noord-Brabant (54.7). Relatively high percentages were found in Zeeland (96) and Utrecht (89.3). Provinces with relatively low percentages of visiting maternity care were Zeeland (3.4) and Gelderland (6.2). Relatively high percentages were found in Groningen (37.8) and Drente (28.2). (In Utrecht the percentage of visiting maternity care was 9.0 and in Noord-Brabant it was 24.6). There was a noticeably high percentage of combined internal and visiting maternity care in Noord-Brabant (20.7 %). In the other provinces this percentage was considerably lower. (In Utrecht it was 0.8 %).

In 1966, about $1^1/_2$ % of the organized domiciliary care was in the form of after-care following a hospital delivery with a 1-3 day stay. In 1970, the percentage of organized domiciliary care after a hospital delivery rose to 4.87 % (absolute figure 5923).

Hospital
As shown by the following table, the number of hospital confinements has risen.

Number of hospital confinements (source GHI)

1961	1965	1966	1967	1968	1969
64,996	69,545	74,445	78,950	82,327	91,824

The number of deliveries with a stay of 0 days (delivery in the delivery room not followed by admission to the ward, the so-called out-patient deliveries) and the deliveries with a nursing period of 1-3 days (the so-called short-stay deliveries) had increased in recent years. However, the foregoing instances represent but a small proportion of the total number of intramural deliveries. In 1968 it was almost 4 %.

The average length of stay in hospital for a maternity patient has fallen slightly. The following table shows the average number of days over a number of years.

1957	1959	1961	1963	1965	1967	1968	1969	1970
11.87	11.84	11.74	11.62	11.44	10.99	11.00		

On the strength of Dutch statistics from 1968 Fokkens (1969) found that there was a certain constancy in the average length of stay that was not to be observed in the number of admissions. There were big differences in the number of admissions for uncomplicated confinements; smaller differences in those for complicated ones.

Feldstein (1967) found that in England, the occupation of maternity beds was chiefly dependent on the number of admissions rather than on the average length of stay. This surprised him in view of the relatively long stay in English hospitals compared with that in the United

17

States. The number of beds available seemed hardly to affect the average length of stay. When the pressure of demand increased, the suppliers did not react to it by admitting larger numbers of patients, nor did they reduce the average length of stay as a means of establishing a balance between demand and supply. The same might be said of the Netherlands. It seems that here too, as in England, a nursing period of 10 to 11 days following a delivery is a firmly-rooted custom. A comparison between the resulting situation in Holland with that in the United States might lead to some important conclusions with regard to the number of beds required.

In 1964, the number of available cots for healthy infants was practically the same as in 1959. In 1969 there were 11.3 % more than in 1964 (GHI 1970). The total number of hospital beds in the Netherlands in 1964 was 8.4 % more than in 1959. In 1969, it was 16.5 % more than in 1964. Thus, the increase in the number of hospital beds was considerably greater than the increase in the number of cots for healthy infants.

The number of hospital beds per 1000 inhabitants increased from 4.78 in 1960 to 5.17 in 1968. The number of cots per 1000 inhabitants remained constant in those years. (0.24).

The fact that the number of cots shows little variation has probably to do with the shortening of the average period of maternity nursing in hospital. No doubt, also, more efficient use is being made of the cots available.

A possible development that might be expected to take place in the field of maternity services is towards the creation of 'obstetrical centres'. Experiments in this direction are now in progress. Deliveries in such a centre may be conducted either by the patient's own family doctor or by a midwife. A gynaecologist will be consulted during the antenatal period to ascertain, amongst other things, whether an uncomplicated delivery is to be expected. If this proves to be the case, patients may choose to be confined either at home or at the obstetrical centre. In both instances, delivery at home and delivery in the obstetrical centre, the centre is the supplier of the services including internal care and visiting care. Patients will, moreover, be given an alternative choice of short-stay admission to the centre, followed by domiciliary after-care.

If this development continues, it will mean greater variety in the package of services offered in respect of normal deliveries. This concept of maternity services is something new in the Netherlands and it is expected to bring about the following benefits: better selection with regard to the use of maternity services, better antenatal care and better opportunities for organized maternity care.

3. PLACE WHERE THE DELIVERY TAKES PLACE

The favourable results produced by the maternity services are all the more remarkable in that they were achieved in the framework of what many people consider to be a 'primitive' pattern of services. By primitive is meant that most confinements take place in the home. However, the following table shows that this situation is changing.

Births in percentages according to place of confinement. (C.B.S. 1971)

	1958	1963	1966	1967	1968	1969	1970
Home	74	70	66	64	62	60	57
Hospital or Maternity home	26	30	34	36	38	40	43
Total number	240,888	253,506	242,746	241,594	239,811	250,340	241,500

The decrease in domiciliary services is not of the same magnitude in all parts of the country. Hospitalization increases with the size of the town. (Verbrugge 1968).

In 1955, the World Health Organization deliberated on the question of where confinements take place. The following is an extract from a publication on the subject (Bridgeman 1955):
'It is here that the crucial problem arises: should home confinements be encouraged, or should each village be provided with a few beds for maternity care'. Finland and the Baltic states were mentioned as 'examples of advanced populations, where confinements at home are clearly preferable to systematic hospitalization'. No mention is made of the Dutch solution.

In the Netherlands, the percentage of hospital deliveries is comparatively low. In Norway and the United States, practically all deliveries take place in clinics.
On the other hand, there is a number of countries such as England and Denmark, where a not inconsiderable proportion of deliveries takes place in the home.
An enquiry carried out under the auspices of the Council of Europe in 1963 showed that in most of the member countries, there was a

19

movement towards institutional deliveries (Goodman 1963). In various countries, institutional deliveries are encouraged (Belgium, France, Italy). There was only one country, Ireland, where domiciliary confinements were encouraged, one of the incentives being exemption from payment of certain expenses.

In England, where in 1966 24% of the deliveries still took place in the home, (in 1968 15%), the place where maternity services are carried out has been the subject of lengthy discussion. Many publications have appeared in the past few years. (Department of Health and Social Security 1970, Baird 1969, Stallworthy 1969, Stearn and Fisher 1968, Peel 1968, Cookson 1967 and others). Facts about a possible preference on the part of the public were hardly mentioned in the discussion until the second half of the nineteen-sixties. One exception to this was the report of an enquiry made amongst women who had been delivered once in hospital and once at home. (Gordon 1960).

The absence of knowledge about patients' preferences was criticized in the following manner (Gordon, page 53):

'There is no doubt at all that most specialist/obstetricians, a few family doctors, and even some medical officers of health are quite unaware that mothers generally are not anxious to be confined in hospital for their second, later, and uncomplicated pregnancies if home conditions are suitable. This lack of awareness is understandable in the specialist obstetrician, pre-occupied with the abnormal cases daily confronting him in his hospital practice and lacking the time and opportunity for continued familiarity with the social and emotional aspects of normal confinement, but the other groups have less excuse for such ignorance.'

In the last few years, various publications have appeared giving the findings of evaluation-enquiry into the supply of maternity services. (Bradford Group General Practitioners, 1966, Galloway 1968, Topliss 1970, Russel and Miller 1970 and Richards, Donald and Hamilton 1970). Among the subjects dealt with were those concerned with the patients' wishes. In general, the patients appeared satisfied with the way their confinement had been arranged, whether it had been a domiciliary confinement, an institutional confinement with a post-natal stay of 8 to 10 days, or a hospital confinement with early discharge.

Preference on the part of the English public was clearly a reflection of actual experience. The conclusion to be drawn from the various evaluation enquiries in England is that public preference can be manipulated and that it conforms to the possibilities that are actually being offered or to indications which entail special arrangements.

20

Several publications have been issued in the Netherlands in the past ten years, in which both advocates and opponents of the continuation of domiciliary confinements expressed their views. The advocates included De Haas-Postuma (1962), Kloosterman (1966 and 1967) and Verbrugge (1968). Among the opponents were Eskes (1967), Rottinghuis (1968) and Seelen (1970).

It should not be thought that advocates of domiciliary confinements ignore the value of hospitals in the scheme of maternity services. They undoubtedly recognize the desirability of hospital assistance but only in cases medically or socially indicated. Strict selection of patients at risk and their referral to hospital are essential for the operation of a system of services which allows the possibility of domiciliary confinements. Those who feel that domiciliary confinements should continue, presuppose that family doctors and midwives must be considered as competent to assume the responsibility for this selection.

Kloosterman (1967) pointed out the psychological benefits of a domiciliary confinement. 'A woman giving birth to a child at home is obviously the centre-point of the whole proceeding'.

'Its physiological character is emphased by the acceptance of the fact that a normal confinement can take place in the home.'

This means, in fact, that domiciliary confinements can make some contribution in respect of mental health. Kloosterman remarks that the existence of domiciliary confinements means that gynaecologist/obstetricians can continue to concentrate their activities on obstetrical pathology. He continues:

'To direct all obstetrical work to the hospitals and to place it in the hands of highly-specialized, university-trained people is a social mismanagement that, on grounds of efficiency, economy, in short, on the grounds of making the most effective use of available human energy, cannot be sufficiently condemned.'

The most important medical argument put forward by protagonists of hospitalization is that it can never be ascertained in advance whether a delivery will proceed without complications. Statistics concerning unexpected complications, referral percentages and secondary hospitalization are given by de Haas-Postuma (1962), Pel and Pel-Mellink (1962), Kloosterman (1967), Verboom (1968), Swaak (1968) and Verbrugge (1968).

Obstetrical skill is, in principle, most continuously available in hospital. Yet, even there, it is possible for babies to be born without the presence of a doctor or midwife (NHG 1966). Out of 9569 single births there were 511 births in which the final phase of expulsion occurred without obstetrical assistance. 5.9% of these were domiciliary confinements, 4.1% were hospital deliveries on social indication, and 3.1% were hospital deliveries on medical indication.

Rottinghuis (1968) was of the opinion that domiciliary deliveries were to be defended particularly on grounds of a number of factors connected with a negative impression of hospitals. In his view, the main factors were the patient's fear of hospital (the use of the word 'patient' is significant), the idea that hospitals are intended for pathology, and the danger of infection in hospitals. Rottinghuis assumes that these negative factors can be eliminated.

4. PRICES AND TURNOVER OF MATERNITY SERVICES IN 1971

Family doctor
For maternity services to compulsorily insured patient (ziekenfonds see page 5) family doctors received the sum of 258.02 guilders from the ziekenfonds in 1971. Besides this, 23.61 guilders per delivery were made over to their account with the 'Stichting Voorlopig Beheer van Pensioengelden voor Huisartsen' – a society for administering doctors' pension funds. Thus, the total amount paid to a doctor for maternity services is 281.63 guilders. It is divided into three parts for antenatal care, management of delivery and after-care. If any one of these is not carried out, as might be the case if delivery takes place in hospital, payment is then made according to a differential scale. Separate charges are made for specific operations such as suturing and removing the placenta.

A compulsorily insured woman is entitled to reimbursement of a doctor's fee only if there is in her district no midwife associated with the ziekenfonds or if, for medical reasons, the ziekenfonds authority has given permission for a family doctor to be called for. In the case of voluntarily insured women reimbursement is made for doctor's services even when there is a midwife associated with the ziekenfonds available and though there may be no medical necessity. However, the amount paid is only the equivalent of what the ziekenfonds would otherwise have paid to the midwife.

The fee charged by the doctor to patients other than those insured by the ziekenfonds is, in principle, determined by himself as a member of an independent profession. The National Association of General Practitioners recommends a fee equal to 20 times the fee for a single visit or 20 times the fee for a surgery consultation. 17 and 12 guil-

22

ders respectively. Thus, on a basis of these recommendations, the fee for antenatal, natal and postnatal services was 340 to 300 guilders. (Later calculations will presuppose an average of 320 guilders). In practice, the doctor is able to use the amount of his fee as a means of moderating demand.

Midwife

In 1971, midwives received 200 guilders from the ziekenfonds for conducting a delivery (including antenatal and postnatal care). Moreover, the ziekenfonds contributed the sum of 13.40 guilders per delivery (6.7 % of the fee) to the midwives' pension funds. This brought the cost per delivery to 213.40 guilders. Midwives are free to fix their own fees for attending confinements of privately insured patients and these are often somewhat higher than those paid by the ziekenfonds. In fact, privately insured women seldom use the services of a midwife.

Specialist

With regard to ziekenfonds insured women who, for medical reasons, were admitted to hospital (3rd class), the gynaecologist was paid 240 guilders per patient in 1971 for antenatal, natal and postnatal care. A further sum of 17.28 (7.2 % of the fee) was contributed to the pension-funds thus bringing the total cost of the delivery to 257.28 guilders. In the case of privately insured women, the specialists agreed among themselves as to how their fees should be calculated, viz. for a delivery without medical indication (including antenatal and postnatal care) 3rd class, 540 guilders; for a delivery in the same class but with medical indication 648 guilders.

Fees for attendance of private patients in class 2B were $1^1/_2$ times those for class 3 (810 and 972 guilders respectively), and for class 2A they were twice as much as those for class 3 (1080 and 1296 guilders respectively). The recommendations allow for a variation in the above amounts of 25 %. There are no recommendations as to fees for patients 1st class.

Hospital

Charges for hospital services are based on cost-prices. No difference is made with regard to the various departments or units nor as to the degree of service provided. In accordance with the law governing the rate of hospital charges, prices are controlled by the Central Office for Hospital Tariffs.

There are often big differences in the prices charged for their services

23

by different hospitals. This analysis is based on average prices according to information obtained from the Central Office for Hospital Tariffs.

In 1970, the average hospital-fee 3rd class was 66.16 guilders per day. The controlling body expects an average increase in 1971 of 21.4%. This means that in 1971, the average price for hospital services 3rd class will be 80.32 guilders per day. This includes an approximate amount of 5 guilders for the use of an operating theatre, medicines and clinical laboratory tests (in the so-called 'all-in, not including doctor deal' plus the cost of any specialist attention that may be required in an 'all-in, doctor included deal'). With the exception of the all-in deal, the average price of a stay in hospital 3rd class was 75.32 guilders per day.

To calculate the average price for classes 2/2B the sum must be multiplied by 1.3 (97.92 guilders) and for classes 1/2A by 1.65 (124.28 guilders). 40 guilders is charged for the use of the delivery room and 150 guilders for an outpatient delivery irrespective of the category for which the patient is insured. The hospital charges for a healthy infant half the price that the mother has to pay for 3rd class accommodation i.e. 37.66 guilders per day in 1971.

The charge for sick babies (e.g. those needing incubator nursing) is that for normal 3rd class accommodation.

Maternity Homes
Maternity homes are not covered by the law concerning hospital charges and are not therefore, subject to control by the Central Office for Hospital Tariffs.

Halfway through 1971 we looked into the rates charged by the 22 recognized maternity homes, including 2 obstetrical centres. Calculation of the average price to be paid for accommodation in a maternity home was based on the tariff for mother *and* child, including the use of the delivery room and a stay of 10 days. 12 of the 22 homes kept to a nursing and care period of 10 days; 1 to a period of 9 to 10 days; 6 to a period of 9 days; 2 to a period of 8 to 9 days. 1 home was unable to state the average length of stay. 14 of the homes had 1 standard tariff, 3 of them had different tariffs for 1st and 2nd class, while 5 of them had 3 different classes and tariffs. The average price for a stay of 10 days in a maternity home for mother and child was 666.41 guilders (calculated on the lowest class and the standard class).

In the case of homes that offer accommodation at various prices, the average of these prices is higher by 40.91 guilders (707.32 guilders).

Organized maternity care
The rates charged for maternity care are based on cost prices. There are often considerable differences in the prices charged by different centres. On January 1st 1971, the average price for internal maternity care was 728 guilders for a stay of 10 days (calculated from information obtained from the White/Yellow Cross Society and from the Limburg Green Cross Society). This was an increase of 62% compared with 1968. The average price for visiting maternity care was 292 guilders for 10 days, an increase of 67% on 1968).

Prices for a combination of services
The following table shows the most prevalent combinations of maternity services and the average prices relating to them (in guilders). Where necessary, differentiation has been made between prices that apply to compulsorily insured women (Z) and those that concern the privately insured (P).

Domiciliary deliveries
a. Family doctor + 10 days internal maternity care   Z   1009.63
                                                              P   1048.—
b. Family doctor + 10 days visiting maternity care   Z   573.63
                                                              P   612.—
c. Midwife + 10 days internal maternity care   Z   941.40
d. Midwife + 10 days visiting maternity care   Z   505.40

Deliveries in maternity homes
e. Family doctor + 10 days nursing/care mother and   Z   948.04
   child + hotel services and including use of delivery   P   986.41
   room[1]
f. Midwife + 10 days nursing/care mother and child   Z   879.81
   + hotel services and including use of delivery room[1]

Deliveries in hospital
g. 3rd class: specialist (no medical indication) + 10   1709.80
   days nursing/care mother and child + hotel services
   and delivery room
h. idem with medical indication for hospital treatment   Z   1427.08
                                                                P   1817.80

1. Based on the price of standard class and lowest class in maternity home. For cost including higher prices of higher classes, the amounts Z and P should be increased by 40.91 guilders each.

i.	same as g., in class 2/2B		2205.80
j.	same as h., in class 2/2B		2367.80
k.	same as g., in class 1/2A		2739.40
l.	same as h., in class 1/2A		2955.40
m.	3rd class: family doctor + 10 days nursing/care	Z	1451.43
	mother and child + hotel service and delivery room	P	1489.80
n.	same as m., in class 2/2B		1715.80
o.	same as m., in class 1/2A		1979.40
p.	3rd class: midwife + 10 days nursing/care mother		1384.20
	and child + hotel services + delivery room		
q.	same as p., in class 2/2B		1608.20

The following cost elements should be taken into account when calculating the cost of a short-stay or outpatient hospital delivery followed by domiciliary after-care: cost of managing delivery (family doctor, midwife or specialist), cost of outpatient delivery or cost of nursing mother and child for the duration of their stay in hospital (plus the use of the delivery room), and the cost of the supplementary internal maternity care or visiting maternity care.

It may be concluded, on the strength of the above figures, that a domiciliary confinement is cheaper than a hospital confinement. There is a difference of over 300 guilders between the most expensive combination of domiciliary services (a) and the cheapest combination of hospital services (p).

The difference in cost between the most expensive package of domiciliary services and a hospital delivery with specialist attention is anything between 400 to 800 guilders in 3rd class, 1200 to 1300 guilders in class 2/2B and 1700 to 1900 guilders in class 2A/1! Delivery in a maternity home with 3rd class nursing is slightly cheaper than domiciliary delivery with internal maternity care.

In the case of domiciliary deliveries, the cost of purchasing certain articles such as maternity mattress, towels etc. must be taken into account besides, too, the cost of feeding mother and child.

Extra considerations in the case of hospital or maternity home deliveries are travelling expenses and the costs involved in caring for the rest of the family during the mother's absence. The cost of feeding mother and child at home is eliminated.

Turnover of maternity services
Calculation of the turnover of maternity services by the various sup-

pliers in 1971, was based on the figure of 240,000 births (in 1970 241.677) (source CBS).

If the situation continues to develop as in the previous years, we shall find in 1971, that 56 % of deliveries will take place in the home and 44 % in institutions (hospitals and others). This represents in absolute figures 134,400 and 105,600. According to figures provided by the Chief Inspector of Public Health, the number of births in recognized maternity homes in 1970 was 7,624 (in non-recognized homes in 1968 there were 1,811). It is estimated that in 1970, the number of births in homes other than hospitals will be about 9,000. Thus the number of births taking place in Dutch hospitals will be 96,600.

In 1969, 63 % of the confinements were managed by doctors, 37 % by midwives. There was little change in the respective percentages from 1963 to 1967. After 1967, more of the work devolved on the midwives. It is anticipated that in 1971, 62 % of confinements will be managed by a doctor and 38 % by a midwife; in absolute figures 148,800 and 91,200 respectively. According to the Council for Medical Registration, in 1970 80 % of the deliveries that took place in affiliated hospitals were managed by specialists. From this percentage it is anticipated that in 1971, specialists will manage about 77,280 births. Since the number of deliveries conducted by specialists outside the hospital is negligible, this may be taken to be the total turnover of specialist assistance at confinements.

The number of births conducted by family doctors will, on the basis of the foregoing figures, amount to about 71,520 in 1971.

These calculations do not take into account confinements managed by 'others'. In the field research, this applied in particular to doctors assisting specialists and to medical students in teaching hospitals. According to the Council for Medical Registration, 0,2 % of deliveries that took place in their affiliated hospitals in 1969 were managed by 'others', and 0,4 % in 1970.

In 1970 the maternity centres took 121,539 bookings, of which 78.4 % (95,335) were for internal care, 15.1% (18,366) for visiting care and 6.4 % (7.838) for a combination of services. A slight drop in numbers is to be expected in 1971 equal to that in 1970 compared with 1969. Thus, the number of maternity bookings in 1971 will be about 115,000. Divided in the same proportions, this means that there will be 90,160

27

for internal care, 17,365 for visiting care and 7,360 for a combination of services.

Turnover of maternity services

The turnover of maternity services in 1971 was roughly estimated as follows (in guilders × 1000):

Family doctor	71,520 (50% at ƒ 281.63; 50% at ƒ 320,—[2])	= 21,500
Midwife	91,200 (100% at ƒ 213.40)	= 19,500
Specialist	77,280 (70% at ƒ 257.28; 30% at ƒ 900.—[2])	= 34,800

Organized maternity care

Internal care[3]	93,850 at ƒ 728.—	68,300
Visiting care[3]	21,050 at ƒ 292.—	6,100
Maternity Home	9,000 50% at ƒ 666.41 (50% at ƒ 707.32)	6,200
Hospital	96,600	
Nursing/care	60% in 3rd class at ƒ 1129,80;	
	30% in class 2/2B at ƒ 1355.80;	
	10% in class 2A/1 at ƒ 1619.40[4]	120,400
Delivery room (100% at ƒ 40.—)		3,900
Total		280,700

It must be emphasized that the sum of around 280 million guilders does not represent the total cost of maternity services but only those costs that can be charged to individuals. No account has been taken in this case of training (midwives, maternity helps etc.) nor of any kind of subsidies (e.g. for the management of maternity centres). Neither has consideration been given to extra costs such as those concerning transport by ambulance, anaesthetization, incubator care, average length of stay exceeding 10 days etc. Other expenses not included in the calculation are those incurred by the consumer in the purchase of material, extra nourishment, extra domestic help, travelling expenses in cases of non-domiciliary confinement.

On the strength of the foregoing figures it is estimated that a shortening of the nursing/care period by one day would mean a saving of 20 million guilders. (10% of the cost of maternity care and admission to hospital or maternity home). A reduction in the average period of

2. Average price of services to privately insured patients.
3. Including half of the cases involving a combination of services.
4. For mother and child assuming that the child is healthy.

28

nursing/care in hospital alone (11 days in 1968) would save 12.5 million guilders.

If one day of internal domiciliary care or nursing/care in a maternity home were to be substituted for one day in hospital, a saving would be effected of approximately 5 million guilders a year. If all deliveries were to take place in hospital with an average stay of 10 days and without any increase in the number managed by specialists, there would be an extra cost of about 100 million guilders a year.

Premium for ziekenfonds and private insurances
Part of the cost of maternity services is not paid directly by the consumer, but is covered by the ziekenfonds and private insurances. Eventually, however, the consumer does pay even for that part, in the form of premiums. In most cases, the employer also contributes to these premiums. This contribution may be regarded as a portion of his income that is paid out by the employee in a fixed form.

In 1971, the premium for compulsory (ziekenfonds) insurance was 7.7% of the wage (with a maximum of 1102 guilders) and half of it was paid by the employer. In 1971, is was established by the Consumers' Association that the average annual premium for voluntary ziekenfonds insurance was 1145 guilders. The wage limit, i.e. the maximum wage that permits participation in the ziekenfonds whether compulsorily or voluntarily, was 17,150 guilders in 1971. According to the findings of the Consumers' Association, a privately insured couple without children paid a premium of 940 guilders a year (average) and a couple with three children paid on an average 1620 guilders.

29

Sketch plan of maternity services

Services offered by:	Maternity services		
	Antenatal care	Natal care	Postnatal care
General practitioner	– examination of pregnant women (incl. selection of women at risk) – supervision of pregnancy – therapeutic activities if required (general medical care) – information, instruction – referral to a specialist if necessary	– obstetric assistance	– examination of mother and child – information and instruction – therapeutic activities where necessary
Midwife	– examination of pregnant women – supervision of pregnancy (providing that this is a normal one; selection of women at risk) – information, instruction – referral to general practitioner or specialist if necessary	– obstetric assistance	– examination and supervision – information and instruction
Specialist	– examination ⎫ – supervision ⎬ women at risk and pathology – therapy in ⎭ some cases – specialized (medical care)	– obstetric assistance	– examination and supervision – therapeutic activities where necessary
Maternity centre (Cross organization)	– instruction (individual or in classes for mothercraft or parentcraft) – maternity exercises	– assistance at delivery by (student) maternity help – availability of equipment such as bedblocks, bedpan etc.	'internal' maternity care: – nursing/care of mother and child – observation – instruction – housekeeping 'visiting' maternity care: – nursing and care of mother and child (one or twice a day)
Maternity home		– suitable accommodation including delivery room – assistance by maternity nurses/maternity helps	– nursing/care of mother and child – accommodation – hotel services
Hospital	– diagnostic facilities – therapeutic facilities	– suitable accommodation – properly equipped delivery room – availability of facilities such as: operating theatre, blood bank, qualified staff – '24 hours a day service' – In case of an outpatient delivery discharge from hospital within 24 hours	– nursing/care of mother and child – availability of facilities – '24 hours a day service' – hotel services – In cases of short-stay deliveries, generally one to three days
Obstetric centre (as yet in development)	– for examination of pregnant women by general practitioner or midwife, a gynaecologist is also consulted	a. domiciliary deliveries: – assistance by (student) maternity help b. delivery in an obstetric centre: – assistance by (student) maternity help – suitable accommodation including delivery room	ad a. – same as for internal district maternity care ad b. – same as for maternity home (if desired short-stay delivery followed by maternity care at home)

3. Findings of the field research

The information obtained from the 400 respondents concerned their experience of maternity services and their opinions regarding these services. The information threw significant light on the consumers' 'market behaviour'.

1. ENTERING THE MARKET

Table 1. First contact. With whom contact was first established as a result of pregnancy

	Total (%) group	Utrecht	Tilburg	Rural area Utrecht	Rural area Tilburg
Family doctor	72	58	69	83	77
Midwife	9	8	18	2	9
Specialist	6	8	7	6	3
Cross Society	5	4	1	7	9
Organon (Pharmaceutics)	5	15	5	–	–
Other	3	7	–	2	2
Total number	400	100	100	100	100

In the rural area, demand was directed mostly to the family doctor. In Tilburg, a relatively large number of women consulted the midwife in the first place. In the rural areas more than in the towns, contact was first sought with the Cross Societies which supply domiciliary maternity care. In Utrecht a relatively large number of women contacted the pharmaceutical firm of Organon in connection with their 'Mothers for Mothers' campaign. This is a scheme by which urine is collected regularly from pregnant women for the manufacture of a fertility preparation.

31

Table 2. The stage of pregnancy at which the first contact was made (in percentages).

1 st mth.	2nd mth.	3rd mth.	4th mth.	5th mth.	6th to 9th mth.	Total number
15	45	27	11	2	1	400

Relatively the largest number of women had their first contact in connection with their pregnancy in the 2nd month.

There was only slight difference in respect of the timing of the first contact, between urban and rural areas and between the provinces of Brabant and Utrecht.

Prenatal care

Seven of the women involved in the enquiry said they had had no prenatal care.

The percentage of women who had had prenatal care from their family doctor or midwife was greater than the number whose delivery was managed by the family doctor or midwife. This was a result of referral to a specialist.

Table 3. The start of prenatal care (in percentages)

Unknown	1st mth.	2nd mth.	3rd mth.	4th mth.	5th mth.	6th to 9th mth.	had no prenatal care	Total number
1	7	31	35	18	4	2	2	400

In most cases prenatal care started in the 3rd, 2nd or 4th month. 91% of the women had received prenatal care before the 5th month. No connection could be indicated between the timing of the first request for prenatal care and the age of the woman, her religion, her education or her husband's profession.

Frequency of prenatal care

As shown by table 4, a relatively large number of women had been for a check-up 9 or 10, 7 or 8 and 5 or 6 times. Relatively few had had but few examinations (1 or 2, and 3 or 4) 10 % of the respondents had had 15 or more prenatal examinations.

Table 4. Number of antenatal examinations (in percentages)

Not known	None	1-2	3-4	5-6	7-8	9-10	11-12	13-14	15 and more	Total number
–	2	1	2	18	24	30	9	4	10	400

In general, the specialist carried out more antenatal examinations than the family doctor and the midwife; the family doctor carried out more than the midwife. This is not surprising in view of the fact that doctors, particularly specialists, are called on to attend in cases of pregnancy where complications might be expected. The risk of, or the existence of complications necessitates more frequent use of prenatal services. The number of prenatal examinations makes no difference to the fee.

The final choice in the package of maternity services may be influenced by conversations the consumer has had or by advice she has been given. In order to find out who had exerted the influence the respondents were asked with whom they had discussed the matter of who should attend them and where. More than 40 % of the respondents said that they had talked with their husbands about who should conduct the delivery and where it should take place. A quarter of the women had talked with no-one about it. A quarter of them had discussed the matter with their family doctor. Considerably fewer women had consulted other persons. As a rule, the discussion was not in the nature of definite advice. 78 % of the women said that they had received no advice as to who should conduct the delivery. 10 % had been advised by their family doctor. Advice from others had been given only sporadically. More advice had been given on the matter of where delivery should take place. In 15 % of the cases it came from the family doctor and this applied particularly to advice to be delivered in hospital. 66 % of the women had received no advice as to where they should be delivered.

With regard to a possible subjection to influence in the demand for maternity services, a number of statements were submitted to the respondents who were asked to common on them.

There was about equal agreement and disagreement with the statement: 'The doctor has the last word in who is to conduct the delivery'. 50 % agreed and 48 % disagreed.

This does not appear to correspond entirely with the opinions on the statement 'Husband and wife have the final decision in how the delivery is to be arranged'. Most of the respondents thought that the husband and wife had the last word. 89 % agreed with the statement as against 10 % who disagreed. The 'choice' as to who should conduct the delivery seemed to have presented no problem as far as the women were concerned. Only 2 % supported the statement: 'We found it difficult to decide whom to choose to conduct the delivery'. The great majority of 95 % said that was not the case.

2. MANAGEMENT OF DELIVERY

a. *By whom this was carried out*
The following table shows who managed deliveries and where. The 4 areas where research was carried out are listed separately, viz. Utrecht, Tilburg, rural district Utrecht and rural district Tilburg.

Table 5. Supplier of maternity management according to research area and place of delivery

	Home	Maternity home	Hospital	Other
Utrecht				
Family doctor	18	6	1	–
Midwife	26	4	3	–
Specialist	–	–	21	–
Other	4	1	12	–
Combination	–	–	4	–
Total number	48	11	41	–
Tilburg				
Family doctor	10	5	–	–
Midwife	31	16	–	–
Specialist	1	–	35	–
Other	–	1	–	–
Combination	–	–	–	1
Total number	42	22	35	1
Rural area Utrecht				
Family doctor	64	–	8	–
Midwife	6	–	1	–
Specialist	–	1	15	–
Other	1	–	–	–
Combination	3	–	–	1
Total number	74	1	24	1
Rural area Tilburg				
Family doctor	51	–	1	1
Midwife	20	–	–	–
Specialist	–	1	23	–
Other	1	–	–	–
Combination	2	–	–	–
Total number	74	1	24	1

34

Most of the domiciliary deliveries in Utrecht and Tilburg were managed by a midwife: those in the rural areas of Utrecht and Tilburg by a family doctor.

As was to be expected, most of the hospital deliveries were managed by a specialist. The deliveries in Utrecht listed in the category 'other' are those that were attended by specialists' assistents or medical students in the University Hospital, Utrecht. The number of hospital deliveries attended by a family doctor or midwife was relatively small.

b. *The choice of maternity management*

Of the 97 cases where delivery was conducted by a specialist, the initiative to call on the specialist's help came in 72 cases from the family doctor, in 19 cases from the respondent herself and in 10 cases from the midwife. Only 3 of the women had sought specialist's help when it was not considered by the family doctor to be necessary.

The respondents were asked how they had arrived at the 'choice' of a particular specialist. In 46 cases he had been named by the family doctor and in 28 cases by the woman herself. In 23 cases there had been no question of chosing; it was purely a matter of chance.

There were differences between Utrecht, Tilburg, rural area Utrecht and rural area Tilburg.

Table 6. The 'choice' of one particular specialist

	Utrecht	Tilburg	Rural area Utrecht	Rural area Tilburg
Specialist named by family doctor	6	20	9	11
Specialist chosen by the patient herself	5	9	3	11
Specialist named by midwife	–	6	–	2
Specialist engaged fortuitously	16	–	6	1
Total number	27	35	18	25

The number of specialists fortuitously selected was noticeably high in Utrecht and the rural area of Utrecht. In nearly all the cases the women concerned were delivered in the University Hospital. In Tilburg it was often the family doctor who named the specialist. In the rural area of Tilburg he was often chosen by the patient herself.

In the case of almost 80 % of the respondents the delivery was conducted as originally planned. In 20 % of the cases this was not so: 13 %

35

had to abandon the idea of having the family doctor, 4% that of having a midwife and 1% of having a specialist to conduct the delivery. There was variation in the stage of pregnancy at which a decision had to be taken to change the plans.

Table 7. *Stage at which plans were changed in respect of who should conduct delivery*

1st or 2nd month	3rd or 4th month	5th or 6th month	7th or 8th month	9th month	during delivery	after delivery
12	10	12	13	11	18	4

In 18 cases the plan was upset while delivery was in progress.

The answers to the question: 'Why was delivery conducted by that person in particular?' indicates the degree to which the respondents considered the choice to be a limited one. Here, reactions differed in the 4 districts concerned.

Table 8. *Reasons why the delivery was conducted by a particular person*

	Utrecht	Tilburg	Rural area Utrecht	Rural area Tilburg
More or less fortuitous	21	6	1	1
Matter of course, there is no-one else	8	4	45	45
Financial reasons-insurance	6	16	2	8
Medical necessity	25	36	19	23
Other reasons	40	38	33	23
Total number	100	100	100	100

In Utrecht a relatively large number of the women said that it was more or less by chance that their delivery had been conducted by any particular person. In Tilburg there were relatively many who said that the choice had been a medical necessity or that there had been financial reasons for it. In the rural areas many of the women said that it had been a matter of course that the person in question should conduct the delivery. ('There was no-one else anyway').

In cases were there had been previous pregnancies the demand for a particular form of maternity management was compared with that on the two previous occasions.

36

Table 9. Conduct of last delivery, last delivery but one and last delivery but two (in percentages)

	Last delivery	Last delivery but one	Last delivery but two
Family doctor	41	45	46
Midwife	27	25	28
Specialist	24	19	14
Other	5	9	9
Combination	3	2	1
Not known	–	–	2
Total number	400	259	110

The family doctor's share in the market had decreased slightly; that of the specialist has increased.

c. *The demand for specific forms of maternity management in the home and in maternity homes*
The question was examined as to whether the demand for a specific form of maternity management was in any way connected with age, parity, education, social level, insurance and income. In view of the small number of deliveries conducted by family doctors and midwives in hospitals (see table 5) the enquiry was limited to deliveries that took place in the home and in maternity homes. Hospital deliveries will be dealt with in detail in Chapter IV under the heading of Council for Medical Registration.

Table 10. Age. Supervision of delivery in the home and in maternity homes according to age (in percentages)

	Younger than 25	25-29	30-34	35 and older
Family doctor	51	58	60	65
Midwife	44	35	33	25
Other	5	7	7	10
Total number	97	99	60	20

The older the patients, the higher the percentage of deliveries in the home and in maternity homes supervised by family doctors and the lower the percentage of those supervised by midwives. In a comparison between urban and rural districts this conclusion applies only to the former and not to the latter. In rural districts the percentage of deliveries supervised by family doctors was high in all age groups (about

75 %) and the percentage of those supervised by midwives was low (between 15 and 20 %).

Table 11. Parity. Supervision of deliveries in the home and maternity homes according to parity (in percentages)

	1 child	2 children	3 children	4 or more children
Family doctor	48	60	57	63
Midwife	46	34	36	30
Other	6	7	8	6
Total number	83	119	44	30

The share in the market of the midwife for deliveries in the home and in maternity homes was greatest in the case of women with 1 child. Here the family doctor's share was least. This applies in both urban and rural areas.

Table 12. Education. Supervision of deliveries in the home and in maternity homes according to standard of education (in percentages)

	Basic and primary education	Further primary and secondary education	Intermediate and higher education
Family doctor	42	61	67
Midwife	51	33	25
Other	7	6	8
Total number	85	155	36

The largest share of the midwife in the market was with respondents who had followed basic or primary education. Her share was considerably less with the respondents who had followed further primary, secondary, intermediate or higher education. The opposite was the case with family doctors. The connection was very obvious in the towns but not so in the rural areas.

Table 13. Social level. Supervision of deliveries in the home and in maternity homes according to social level (in percentages)

	Social level I and II	Social level III and IV	Social level V and VI
Family doctor	77	65	42
Midwife	19	28	51
Other	3	7	7
Total number	31	125	119

38

The higher the occupation of the husband, the bigger the market share of the family doctor and the smaller that of the midwife. This was the case in both urban and rural areas.

Table 14. Insurance. Supervision of deliveries in the home and in maternity homes according to insurance (in percentages)

	Compulsorily insured	Voluntarily insured	Privately insured
Family doctor	46	64	86
Midwife	47	28	7
Other	7	8	8
Total number	184	39	44

Most of the deliveries supervised by midwives in the home and in maternity homes concerned women who were compulsorily insured. In the case of the privately insured her share was only a small percentage of the market. By far the greatest majority of deliveries of privately insured women both in the home and in maternity homes were supervised by family doctors. Comparison of urban and rural areas showed that the connection between type of insurance and supervision of delivery was present in both cases.

There was a noticeable difference in the extent of the demand for the services of a midwife between those with a compulsory insurance and those with a voluntary insurance (resp. 47 and 28 %).

This can probably be explained as follows. Maternity attention by a midwife is included in the benefits provided by the ziekenfonds. If a woman with a voluntary insurance has maternity services from a family doctor, the insurance pays compensation to the amount that would have been paid to a midwife. A woman who is compulsorily insured receives no compensation for maternity services from a doctor unless the insurance has given permission for his services to be used.

Table 15. Income. Supervision of deliveries in the home and in maternity homes according to net income (in percentages)

	less than 650 guilders	650-850 guilders	850-1050 guilders	1050-1250 guilders	1250 guilders and more
Family doctor	52	42	67	63	89
Midwife	44	50	30	30	–
Other	4	8	4	7	11
Total number	48	102	54	27	18

This will happen only if the services are required on medical grounds or in cases where there is no midwife in the place where the woman lives.

The income category 650-850 guilders provided the midwife with her biggest share in the market for deliveries in the home and in maternity homes. It was considerably smaller in the income categories of 1050-1250 guilders. In the category 1250 and over there was no demand at all for the services of a midwife.

The doctor's share in the market was smallest in the income category 650-850 guilders: In each succeeding category it was larger. It was clearly evident that in the towns, the demand for supervision by the family doctor of deliveries in the home or in maternity homes increased with the level of income. In the rural areas the connection was not obvious.

It should be observed that there may be some question of interrelation as, for instance, between age and parity and between standard of education and social level. The connection between income and type of insurance results from the fact that income (wage limit) is the criterium as to whether or not a person may be insured by the ziekenfonds.

d. *Opinions on maternity management*
Satisfaction with the maternity management provided. Enquiry was made into the degree of satisfaction among the respondents with the maternity management provided.

Table 16. Evaluation of the supervision (in percentages)

	(Very) satisfied	Not bad	(Very) dissatisfied	Not known	Total number
Family doctor	96	1	2	1	165
Midwife	94	2	4	–	107
Specialist	95	2	3	–	97

The differences were slight. 2% of the respondents were dissatisfied (or very dissatisfied) with a delivery supervised by a family doctor. The percentage was 4% for delivery by a midwife and 3% for delivery by a specialist.

Of a total of 12 dissatisfied respondents, 10 lived in town and 2 in a rural area. The reasons for dissatisfaction were of a psychological nature, a medical nature or they were not clear. Reasons of a psychological nature were such as 'was too hasty', 'too curt', 'unsym-

40

pathetic', 'paid too little attention'. Amongst medical reasons mentioned were 'left me too long with an infusion', 'did not give me expert attention', 'infection occurred'.

In respect of the last delivery but one, 4 of the 117 women attended by a family doctor, 2 of the 64 attended by a midwife and 8 of the 50 attended by a specialist were dissatisfied with the treatment they had received. In respect of the last delivery but two, 2 out of 51 attended by a doctor, 1 out of 31 attended by a midwife and 2 out of 15 attended by a specialist were dissatisfied.

The number of respondents who were dissatisfied with the last delivery but one and the last delivery but two was too small to judge whether the dissatisfaction had any influence on the more recent choice.

Preference in the matter of supervision of delivery.

The women were asked whom they would have preferred to supervise their delivery if they had been free to choose and assuming that all expenses would be refunded.

Table 17. Actual supervision compared with preference (in percentages)

| | Delivery was supervised by | | |
Preference for	Family doctor	Midwife	Specialist
Family doctor	85	16	27
Midwife	2	70	4
Specialist	10	8	64
Other	3	4	5
Unknown	1	2	–
Total number	165	107	97

Of the women who had been attended by a family doctor, 85 % preferred a family doctor. In respect of midwives and specialists, the percentages were 70 % and 64 % respectively. The connection between the supervision actually experienced and the preference of the women for a specific type of maternity assistance was present in Utrecht, Tilburg, rural area Utrecht and rural area Tilburg.

It also applied to groups classified according to age, parity, religion, education, insurance and income.

200 women expressed a preference for supervision by a family doctor, 86 for a midwife and 92 for a specialist.

As shown by table 18, the most important reason for preferring a

41

family doctor was the fact that he was familiar and trusted. (62 %) The most important reasons for preferring a midwife were previous satisfactory experience with her (38 %) and the fact that she is a woman (23 %). In the case of the specialist it was his special skill that was considered important (40 %) as well as the added medical possibilities resulting from the availability of hospital accommodation and facilities (36 %).

Table 18. *Most important reasons for preferring a family doctor, midwife and specialist respectively (in percentages)*

	Family doctor	Midwife	Specialist
Familiar, trusted	62	5	5
Previous satisfactory experience	9	38	7
Special skill	6	10	40
More medical possibilities	3	–	36
Midwife is a woman	–	23	–
Not included in any of the foregoing categories	13	15	12
Reason unknown	8	10	–
Total number	200	86	92

In general, the respondents did not appear to attribute differing degrees of skill to the family doctor, midwife and specialist. Nevertheless, table 18 shows that 40 % of the women who were attended by a specialist based their preference on his supposedly superior ability.

53 % of the women agreed and 44 % disagreed with the proposition: 'In the absence of expected complications during delivery it does not matter whether it is supervised by a midwife or by a family doctor'.

55 % of the respondents agreed and 41% disagreed with the proposition: 'In the absence of expected complications during delivery it does not matter whether it is supervised by a family doctor or by a specialist'.

40 % of the women were in favour of the proposition: 'A doctor is better able to supervise a delivery than a midwife'. More of them, namely 47 % were against it.

The opinion expressed in the statement: 'A midwife is better able to supervise a delivery than a family doctor', was shared by 24 % of the respondents. A majority of 60 % rejected it.

44 % of the women agreed with the statement: 'A specialist is better able to supervise a delivery than a family doctor'. 45 % disagreed.

In order to obtain further insight into probable differences in valuation amongst the respondents they were asked what they considered a reasonable fee for a family doctor, midwife and specialist for supervising a delivery. 45 % of the respondents thought that the specialist should be paid the most, 37 % thought that all three should receive the same amount, 13 % had a different opinion and 6 % had no opinion at all.

To the question: 'Can you say why you think (or do not think) that there should be a difference in the amount paid?', the following answers were given.

Table 19. Reasons for and against differences in amount paid (in percentages)

Against a difference:	
they do the same work	30
they are all as good as each other	1
other reason(s)	2
no reason given	5
For a difference:	
more study, more training	18
more difficult work	3
more specialized	7
more skilled	11
other reason(s)	11
no reason given	5
Not included in any of the foregoing categories	2
No opinion	6
Total number	400

Those who thought that the fees should all be the same gave as the main reason: 'They all do the same work'. The women who favoured a difference in fees were motivated in particular by the greater amount of study required, by the greater skill and knowledge and by the more specialized nature of the work.

3. THE DEMAND FOR MATERNITY ARRANGEMENTS IN THE HOME, IN MATERNITY
HOMES AND IN HOSPITAL

a. *The use made of maternity arrangements*

*Table 20. Place where delivery took place in the various districts
investigated*

	Total %	Utrecht	Tilburg	Rural area Utrecht	Rural area Tilburg
At home	59.5	48	42	74	74
Maternity home	8.8	11	22	1	1
Hospital	31.0	41	35	24	24
Other (including combinations)	0.8	–	1	1	1
Total number	400	100	100	100	100

60% of the respondents availed themselves of arrangements at home,
(for the whole of the Netherlands in 1970 $\pm$ 58%), 31% made use of
hospital accommodation (for the whole country $\pm$ 38%) and 9% used
a maternity home (for the whole country $\pm$ 4%).

In conformity with the national trend, it was found that, amongst
the population investigated, there had been a lower percentage of
domiciliary deliveries and an increased percentage of hospital deliveries. In respect of the last delivery but two and the last but one the
percentage of domiciliary deliveries were successively 69 and 63. The
percentages of hospital deliveries were 20 and 29.

The literature indicates considerable differences between the big towns
and rural areas with regard to the place chosen for delivery. These
differences became clearly evident in the course of our enquiry. Three
quarters of the deliveries in the rural areas round Utrecht and Tilburg
took place in the home. In Utrecht itself, somewhat less than half the
deliveries were at home and in Tilburg considerably less than half.

Moreover, when categorized according to living conditions, age, parity,
education, social level, income and insurance, the percentage of deliveries in hospitals and maternity homes was in both towns higher than in
the country districts.

Table 21. Living conditions. Satisfaction with dwelling in town and country related to place of delivery (in percentages)

	Town Satis-fied	Town Not bad	Town Dissatis-fied	Country Satis-fied	Country Not bad	Country Dissatis-fied
Home	45	48	44	74	77	78
Maternity home	18	9	15	1	–	–
Hospital	37	39	41	24	24	22
Other	–	4	–	1	–	–
Total number	131	23	46	174	17	9

The difference in the demand for maternity services in the home, in a maternity home and in hospital between those who were satisfied with their living accommodation and those who were not proved to be insignificant.

Age. In all four areas covered by the enquiry, there were relatively most hospital deliveries in the age group 35 years and older.

Table 22. Place of delivery related to investigation area and age

	Utrecht Home	Utrecht Mater-nity Home	Utrecht Hos-pital	Other	Tilburg Home	Tilburg Mater-nity Home	Tilburg Hos-pital	Other
Younger than 25	16	5	14	–	14	12	9	–
25-29	19	3	14	–	16	7	19	–
30-34	11	3	7	–	6	3	2	1
35 and older	2	–	6	–	6	–	5	–
	Rural area Utrecht				*Rural area Tilburg*			
Younger than 25	26	–	8	–	24	–	6	–
25-29	25	–	7	1	27	–	12	1
30-34	16	1	6	–	18	1	1	–
35 and older	7	–	3	1	5	–	5	–

Parity. There was found to be a connection between parity and place of delivery. Relatively the greater number of domiciliary deliveries were of the second or third child. The smallest number were deliveries of first-born children. This connection was apparent in all four areas.

Table 23. *Place of delivery related to investigation area and parity*

| | Utrecht | | | | Tilburg | | | |
	Home	Maternity Home	Hospital	Other	Home	Maternity Home	Hospital	Other
1 child	12	6	16	–	14	13	22	–
2 children	25	3	15	–	16	7	5	–
3 children	7	2	5	–	7	1	3	1
4 and more children	4	–	5	–	5	1	5	–
	Rural area Utrecht				Rural area Tilburg			
1 child	17	–	9	–	21	–	13	–
2 children	35	1	7	–	30	1	6	1
3 children	10	–	5	–	16	–	2	–
4 and more children	12	–	3	1	7	–	3	–

Education. No connection could be found between level of education and place of delivery. There ware fairly big differences in the four areas.

Table 24. *Place of delivery related to investigation area and education*

| | Utrecht | | | | Tilburg | | | |
	Home	Maternity Home	Hospital	Other	Home	Maternity Home	Hospital	Other
Basic and primary education	20	4	20	–	16	9	9	–
Further primary and secondary education	19	5	15	–	18	11	19	–
Intermediate and higher education	9	2	6	–	8	2	7	1
	Rural area Utrecht				Rural area Tilburg			
Basic and primary education	20	–	6	1	15	–	2	–
Further primary and secondary education	47	1	14	–	52	1	18	1
Intermediate and higher education	7	–	4	–	7	–	3	–

Social level. The 'lower' the husband's occupation the larger the number of domiciliary deliveries and the smaller the number of hospital deliveries.

Table 25. Husband's occupation and place of delivery (in percentages)

	Home	Maternity Home	Hospital	Other	Total number
Social level I and II	51	8	42	–	53
Social level III and IV	58	9	31	2	181
Social level V and VI	64	9	28	–	165

When categorized according to area of investigation there were also found to be relatively more hospital deliveries and fewer domiciliary deliveries in the 'higher' occupational groups than in the 'lower' groups.

Table 26. Place of delivery related to investigation area and husband's occupation

	Utrecht				Tilburg			
	Home	Maternity Home	Hospital	Other	Home	Maternity Home	Hospital	Other
Social level I an II	8	3	9	–	5	1	6	–
Social level III and IV	18	6	15	–	12	9	15	1
Social level V and VI	22	2	17	–	25	12	14	–
	Rural area Utrecht				Rural area Tilburg			
Social level I and II	7	–	3	–	7	–	4	–
Social level III and IV	38	1	12	1	37	1	14	1
Social level V and VI	28	–	9	–	30	–	6	–

Income. There was shown to be a connection between income and place of delivery.

Table 27. Net monthly income and place of delivery (in percentages)

	Home	Maternity Home	Hospital	Other	Total number
Less than 650 guilders	67	12	21	–	61
650- 850 guilders	59	11	31	–	147
850-1050 guilders	59	6	33	3	80
1050-1250 guilders	54	10	34	2	41
1250 guilders and more	44	9	47	–	34

In the higher income groups there were relatively fewer domiciliary deliveries and more hospital deliveries. There was a difference of 13 % between the 1050-1250 guilders group and the 1250 guilders and more group. The respondents in this latter group were privately insured. The conclusions applied to all the areas investigated.

Table 28. Place of delivery related to investigation area and net monthly income

	Utrecht				Tilburg			
		Mater-				Mater-		
		nity	Hos-			nity	Hos-	
	Home	Home	pital	Other	Home	Home	pital	Other
Less than 850 guilders	26	4	19	–	22	18	23	–
1250 guilders 850-1250 guilders	16	5	16	–	14	3	7	1
1250 guilders and more	2	2	5	–	5	1	5	–
		Rural area Utrecht				*Rural area Tilburg*		
Less than 850 guilders	38	–	9	–	41	1	7	–
850-1250 guilders	19	1	8	1	20	–	9	1
1250 guilders and more	4	–	2	–	4	–	4	–

Insurance. The number of hospital deliveries was relatively greater amongst privately insured women than amongst those insured by a ziekenfonds.

Table 29. Type of insurance and place of delivery (in percentages)

	Home	Maternity Home	Hospital	Other	Total number
Compulsory ziekenfonds	61	11	28	1	254
Voluntary ziekenfonds	62	7	29	2	55
Privately insured	53	5	41	–	75

In all the areas investigated the number of hospital deliveries amongst privately insured women was relatively greater than amongst the ziekenfonds insured, except in Utrecht where the numbers were proportionally the same. In that area however, there was a relatively large number of ziekenfonds insured women who made use of the maternity services provided by the University Hospital. Women who were in-

48

sured by a ziekenfonds and admitted to a teaching hospital without medical indication were not required to pay their own expenses. The hospital was satisfied with the remuneration that the patient received from the ziekenfonds under the regulations for maternity benefits (in 1970: 41 guilders per day, up to a maximum of 10 days).

Table 30. Place of delivery related to investigation area and type of insurance

	Utrecht				Tilburg			
	Home	Maternity Home	Hospital	Other	Home	Maternity Home	Hospital	Other
Ziekenfonds insured	37	8	30	–	35	21	26	1
Privately insured	9	3	8	–	6	1	6	–
	Rural area Utrecht				Rural area Tilburg			
Ziekenfonds insured	54	1	16	1	63	1	14	1
Privately insured	16	–	7	–	9	–	10	–

In respect of hospital deliveries distinction has been made between those that took place on medical indication and those where there was no such indication.

Table 31. Clinical deliveries of ziekenfonds insured and privately insured women with or without medical indication (in percentages)

	Medical indication	No medical indication	Not known	Total number
Ziekenfonds insured	21	5	2	309
Privately insured	31	7	4	75

The number of privately insured women admitted to hospital on medical indication was 10% higher than that of ziekenfonds insured women. In respect of clinical deliveries without medical indication the difference was very small. The cost of a clinical delivery on medical indication is refunded by the ziekenfonds or by the insurance. This is not so in the case of clinical deliveries without medical indication.

Privately insured women have more financial advantage than those insured with a ziekenfonds from a hospital delivery on medical indication. For a delivery without medical indication the expenses for maternity services (maternity attention, nursing/care etc.) have to be borne by privately insured women. Most health insurances pay benefits for deliveries (average 200 to 300 guilders in 1971) but they are not sufficient to cover all expenses. Maternity management and care are provided for in the ziekenfonds. Arranged according to income the percentages of clinical deliveries with and without medical indication were as follows.

Table 32. Clinical deliveries with and without medical indication according to income (in percentages)

	Medical indication	No-medical indication	Not known	Total number
0- 650 guilders	18	2	2	61
650- 850 guilders	24	5	2	147
850-1050 guilders	20	9	4	80
1050-1250 guilders	27	2	5	41
1250 guilders and more	35	12	–	34

Here the remarkable fact is revealed that the number of clinical deliveries on medical indication is relatively greater in the higher income groups.

b. *Opinions regarding maternity arrangements at home, in a maternity home and in hospital*
Most of the respondents had found the arrangements they had made use of pleasant or very pleasant. A minority had not found them to be so.

Table 33. Experience with deliveries at home, in a maternity home and in hospital (in percentages)

	Very pleasant	Pleasant	Not bad	Not pleasant	Very un-pleasant	Total number
At home	71	24	3	2	1	236
Maternity home	34	54	9	2	–	35
Hospital	44	33	10	10	3	123

95 % of the women had a favourable opinion and 3 % an unfavourable opinion of their delivery at home. 77 % of those who had been delivered in hospital had found it pleasant or very pleasant. 13 % had found it unpleasant and 10 % thought it not bad.

The women who expressed an unfavourable opinion about their hospital delivery did so on the following grounds:

50

a. dissatisfaction with the hospital procedure including complaints such as: too much disturbance 3×, unsatisfactory treatment 2×, poor food 2×, too many rules and regulations, too impersonal 2×, baby too seldom with the mother 1×, too many different nurses 1×, required to spend too much time lying down 1×, husband warned at too late a stage 1×, noisy 1×.
b. personal feelings such as: prefer to be at home, 13×, too unsociable, less homely 6×, strange surroundings 2×, fear of hospitals 1×, feeling of loneliness 1×.

Reasons for disliking domiciliary deliveries were as follows:
too many disturbances (e.g. too many visitors) 6×, (3 of the respondents added, however, that they had after all, quite enjoyed having their baby at home because of the homeliness, the atmosphere of familiar surroundings), preferred hospital 2×, preferred maternity home 1×, preferred outpatient delivery 1×, (go straight home afterwards), no adequate help in the home 1×, complications during delivery 1×.
No connection could be found between dislike of the maternity arrangements experienced and the parity of the mother.

Opinions were also sought in appropriate cases on the two previous deliveries.

Table 34. Experience with the last delivery but one at home in a maternity home and in hospital (in percentages)

	Favourable	Not bad	Not favourable	Not known No opinion	Total number
At home	90	2	7	1	164
Maternity home	70	15	15	–	20
Hospital	63	15	15	8	75

The percentage 'not favourable' was more than twice as high in the case of hospital deliveries as in that of domiciliary deliveries. The number of respondents who replied with 'not bad' was relatively high in the case of hospital deliveries. The number of respondents who expressed a favourable opinion on a domiciliary delivery was 27 % higher than in the case of hospital deliveries.

In respect of the last delivery but two the results were as follows: of the 75 respondents delivered at home, 2 had unfavourable criticism, 1 answered with 'not bad'; of the 22 respondents delivered in hospital 3 answered with 'not favourable' and 4 with 'not bad'.

51

An attempt was made to draw conclusions from an analysis of dissatisfaction with the arrangements made and used for a previous delivery and the choice of specific arrangements for the next one. However, there was insufficient research material to make this possible.

From the answers to the question as to why and in what respect the respondents had or had not found it pleasant to be delivered at home, in a maternity home or in hospital, it was possible to form an impression of what they considered to be positive factors in the matter of where delivery should take place. There were 8 possible answers and the first reason given by each respondent was noted.

Table 35. Factors considered to be important with regard to place of delivery (in percentages)

	Home	*Maternity home*	*Hospital*
Positive:			
sociable atmosphere	31	9	5
family	26	–	–
good care, attention	1	43	27
familiar surroundings	24	3	2
safety, surety	2	14	30
Negative:	5	6	22
not belonging to any of the			
foregoing categories	9	23	12
not known, no opinion	2	3	2
	238	35	124

Important considerations in domiciliary deliveries were considered to be in particular: sociable atmosphere, homeliness (31%) family circumstances (26%), familiar surroundings (24%). A small proportion of the respondents gave a negative response (5%). In respect of maternity institutions, particular importance was attached to good care and attention (43%). In hospital deliveries, safety and surety were considered to be positive factors (30%) as well as good care and attention (27%).

Of the women who had experienced hospital delivery, a relatively high percentage gave a negative response (22%).

The respondents were also asked to give their opinion on the provision of maternity services at home, in hospital and in maternity homes.

The object of this was to form an impression of the women's ideas on the different alternatives and their attitude towards them.

52

Such answers as 'homely', 'more at ease', 'satisfactory care', 'everything within easy reach', 'safe' were noted as positive. Others such as 'not allowed to have any say in matters', 'less homely', 'too wholesale, that puts me off', 'muddly', 'undesirable', were counted as negative answers. Answers such as 'lovely for lying-in but not if there are children', 'nice in the right circumstances', 'if there's no room at home', 'if it's necessary', 'don't mind if I have to' were counted as positive answers with reservations.

When all the answers had been classified, the following results emerged.

Table 36. 'Charge' of opinion on deliveries at home, in maternity homes and in hosiptal (in percentages)

	Home	*Maternity home*	*Hospital*
No opinion given	20	59	23
Positively-charged answer	51	18	30
Positive with reservations	5	2	4
Negatively-charged answer	10	7	15
Not belonging to one of the foregoing categories	15	15	29
	400	400	400

Classification of the answers in this way is a precarious undertaking in view of the great variety of answers and the existence of borderline cases; so the table should be consulted with the necessary reservations.

It shows that there was not much difference in the number of respondents who expressed no opinion about delivery at home or in hospital ($\pm$ 20%). About half the respondents could give no opinion about maternity homes, which was not surprising since many women living in rural areas have never heard of this alternative.

Half the respondents gave positively-charged opinions on domiciliary deliveries as against roughly 30% who responded positively to hospital deliveries. The percentage of women having a negatively-charged opinion on hospital deliveries was somewhat higher than of those having a negative opinion on domiciliary deliveries.

Opinions about the place where deliveries can take place were further investigated on the basis of a number of statements that the women were asked to consider. This also served as a cross-check on the answers already given to some of the questions on the same subject.

38% of the women agreed with the statement that 'When no complications are expected during delivery it makes no difference whether it takes place at home or in hospital'. A good 60% disagreed with the statement.

The majority of the respondents expressed a preference for domiciliary delivery. This is apparent from the reactions to the statement: 'In my opinion delivery should take place at home. Hospital deliveries should remain the exception to the rule'. A good 60% agreed with the statement; 37% disagreed.

The answers concerning the statement 'All deliveries ought to take place in hospital. Those taking place at home should remain the exceptions', reflected the same attitude. 75% disagreed with it and 24% agreed. The statement: 'It is better for the rest of the family if a woman is delivered in hospital' was refuted by a large majority of the women (69%). Those who agreed with the statement amounted to 24%. Reactions to the statement: 'It is pleasanter for a woman to be delivered in hospital than at home' reflected a clear preference for domiciliary deliveries. 64% disagreed with the statement; 31% agreed.

Most of the women had a positive attitude towards safety in hospitals. A majority of 80% agreed with the statement: 'It is safer to be delivered in hospital than at home'. A minority of 18% disagreed.

Preference
In the framework of the enquiry it was important to know the wishes of the women with regard to the provision of maternity services. These wishes were not to be limited by financial, medical or other factors.

The question put before the women in this connection was: 'If you could freely choose to have your delivery at home, in a maternity home, in a hospital or elsewhere and all expenses would be refunded, where would you choose?' 70% of the women preferred to be delivered at home, 19% preferred hospital and 9% preferred a maternity home.

Table 37. Place of delivery and preference (in percentages)

| Preference for | Actual place of delivery | | |
	Home	Maternity home	Hospital
Home	89	26	45
Maternity home	4	54	6
Hospital	6	14	46
Other	1	6	3
Total number	238	35	124

54

As shown in table 37, there was a connection between the place where delivery actually occurred and the preference of the patient.

A great majority (89%) of the women who had been delivered at home expressed a preference for this. Only a small percentage of them would have preferred to be delivered in hospital or maternity home. The percentage of preferences for a hospital delivery amongst women who actually had been delivered in hospital was 46. Only 1% fewer would have preferred delivery at home.

When sub-divided into areas of research the preferences were as follows:

Table 38. Connection between actual place of delivery and preference, arranged according to area of research

Preference for	Home	Maternity home	Hospital	Other
		Delivery took place:		
Utrecht				
Home	43	4	16	–
Maternity home	1	5	1	–
Hospital	2	2	23	–
Other	2	–	1	–
Total	48	11	41	–
Tilburg				
Home	32	3	10	1
Maternity home	6	14	4	–
Hospital	3	3	20	–
Other	1	2	1	–
Total	42	22	35	1
Rural area Utrecht				
Home	68	1	17	1
Maternity home	1	–	1	–
Hospital	5	–	6	–
Other	–	–	–	–
Total	74	1	24	1
Rural area Tilburg				
Home	68	1	13	1
Maternity home	2	–	1	–
Hospital	4	–	8	–
Other	–	–	2	–
Total	74	1	24	1

In all four of the areas investigated a good majority of the women who had been delivered at home actually preferred a domiciliary delivery.

The majority of the women in Tilburg and Utrecht whose delivery took place in hospital preferred a hospital delivery. The situation was different amongst women from the country districts. 17 of the 24 women from the area round Utrecht who had been delivered in hospital would have preferred to be delivered at home. This is also applied to 13 of the 24 women from the area round Tilburg.

The connection between the place where delivery took place and the preference of the women was also apparent when the respondents were categorized according to age, parity, standard of education, social level, income and insurance.

The reasons given for preferring to be delivered in a particular place were much the same as those given for approving of the place where delivery had actually been experienced.

The 279 women who expressed a preference for delivery at home gave as their reason: sociable atmosphere 161 ×, the family 40 ×, own familiar surroundings 24 ×, other reasons 11 ×, no reason given 43 ×. The 36 respondents who preferred a maternity home gave as reason: peace and quiet 12 ×, care and attention 8 ×, other reasons 6 ×. 76 respondents who preferred hospital did so because of: the safety and surety 42 ×, the greater medical possibilities 7 ×, satisfactory experience 10 ×, good care and attention 10 ×, other reasons 6 ×, no reason given 1 ×.

4. NURSING/CARE: IN THE CASE OF DOMICILIARY DELIVERIES

The great majority (88 %) of the women who had been delivered at home had been cared for during confinement by a maternity aid, and 7 % of them by a district nurse. Care during confinement by husband, family or friends/neighbours/acquaintances/occurred seldom (respectively 12 ×, 5 ×, 5 ×. total of 9 %).

Most of the women who had been cared for by a maternity aid (93 %) were satisfied with the attention they had received. 14 of the 210 had complaints about it (7 %). The complaints concerned the care as such e.g. too little attention, inaccurate, unhygienic (11 ×), lack of personal contact (2 ×), being attended too many, namely 4, different maternity aids (1 ×).

In the case of 66 % of the women the confinement period lasted 10 days, of 13 % 9 days, of 11 % 8 days and of 4 % 7 days. 6 % of the women reported a different length of confinement.

85 % of the women delivered at home had been supplied with domes-

tic help as well as maternity care by a maternity aid. The family was involved in providing domestic help in 13 % of the cases. The husbands played but a modest part (7×) as did the home family helps (4×) and the friends/neighbours/acquaintances (3×). 5 women said that they had had no domestic help. The period over which domestic help was given generally lasted for 10 days (66 %); in 10 % of the cases it lasted for 9 days, in 11% of the cases it was 8 days and in 4 % it was 7 days. 9 % of the women delivered at home reported a different period of time.

92 % of the 202 women who had received domestic help from a maternity aid were satisfied with it. 17 % had complaints about it (8 %). All the complaints concerned shortcomings in domestic ability with the exception of one which was about character.

The care for mother and infant plus the housekeeping carried out by a maternity aid involved the respondents in expenses of less than 50 guilders in the case of 17 %, 50 to 100 guilders in the case of 20 %, 100 to 200 guilders for 20 %, 200 to 300 guilders for 11% and upwards of 300 guilders for 14 %. 14 % of the respondents said that care for mother and baby plus domestic help by a maternity aid had involved them in no expenses. 5 % could not say what the costs had been.

In the cases where the cost of care for mother and baby plus domestic help had amounted to less than 200 guilders, the women were insured with a ziekenfonds. The amount the patient had to pay was determined according to a tariff worked out by the maternity centre less the contribution paid by the ziekenfonds.

Home help in the case of institutional deliveries
During the absence of the mother for delivery in hospital or in a maternity home a replacement had to be provided to keep house.

Relatives seem often to have lent a helping hand (40 %) though a fairly large number of the respondents (31%) said that no-one had done the housekeeping while they were away. In these cases the husband and children (if any) had generally gone to stay with relations, thus shifting some of the expenses onto them. In 23 % of the cases the husband had taken over the household duties. In 7 % of the cases other people were involved in running the house including home helps, friends, neighbours and acquaintances.

Of the 162 women who had been delivered away from home, 58 (36 %) said that the housekeeping during their absence had entailed extra expenses, generally in the form of a financial remuneration or for buying a present. These expenses amounted to: less than 50 guil-

57

ders for 11 respondents, between 50 and 100 guilders for 14 of them, between 100 and 150 guilders for 3, between 150 and 200 guilders for 12 and upwards of 200 guilders for 5. 13 of the women did not specify an amount.

Nursing/care in the case of deliveries in hospitals and maternity homes
56 % of the respondents who had been delivered in hospital left there on or between the seventh and tenth day. The largest frequency was on the eighth day (21%). A quite considerable number of the women remained in hospital for longer than 12 days (19 %). These were all cases admitted on medical indications. 7 % of the respondents left hospital within 24 hours.

8 % of them left on or between the first and the sixth day and a further 8 % stayed in hospital for 11 or 12 days.

Of the 35 women who had been delivered in a maternity home 25 stayed there for 9, 10 or 11 days.

Of those delivered in hospital half were in the 3rd class, 40 % in the 2nd class and an insignificant number in the first class. It is not known in which class 10 % were nursed.

The women were asked how many other people were lying with them in the same room or ward. They were also asked with how many people they would have liked to share a room (total number to include themselves). There was an obvious connection between the number of people who had actually shared the room and the number the respondents considered to be desirable. Only a small minority said they would have preferred fewer patients per room than had actually been the case and still fewer would have preferred more.

Table 39. Connection between actual number of co-occupants of hospital/maternity homeward and number considered desirable

		Number preferred					
Actual number	Alone	2 people	3 people	4 people	5/6 people	7 or more	no opinion
Alone	10	3	–	1	3	–	–
2 people	11	22	3	1	1	1	–
3 people	1	3	24	1	1	–	–
4 people	–	1	1	23	1	–	2
5/6 people	–	1	6	2	19	1	1
7 or more	1	1	1	5	1	12	1

The respondents were asked to estimate the cost of the various types of maternity services they had availed themselves of whereby it was emphasized that all costs should be included and not simply those that were not covered by the ziekenfonds or the insurance.

Maternity services (including antenatal and postnatal care)
The cost of maternity services provided by the family doctor was estimated to be: less than 200 guilders 9%, 200 to 300 guilders 38%, 300 to 400 guilders 26%, upwards of 400 guilders 17%. 10% had no idea how much the services had cost.

The services of a midwife were estimated to have cost: less than 200 guilders 29%, 200 to 300 guilders 22%, 300 to 400 guilders 11%, upwards of 400 guilders 3%. 35% had no idea how much the services had cost.

The specialists' services were estimated to have cost: less than 200 guilders 8%, 200 to 400 guilders 17%, 400 to 600 guilders 20%, 600 to 800 guilders 11%, 800 to 1200 guilders 13%, upwards of 1200 guilders 10%. 21% had no idea how much the services had cost.

It is obvious that as regards the midwife and the specialist whose fees, with very few exceptions, are paid entirely by the ziekenfonds or the insurance, a relatively large number of the respondents had no idea as to how much the fee had amounted to. There was less insight into these expenses because they were paid by ziekenfonds or insurance.

Services of the maternity aid
The cost of the services supplied by the maternity aid in caring for mother and baby and doing the housekeeping were estimated at: less than 200 guilders 18%, 200 to 400 guilders 19%, 400 to 600 guilders 35%, upwards of 600 guilders 17%. 11% had no opinion.

Services of hospital and maternity home
The respondents who had been delivered in hospital estimated the cost (nursing/care, hotel services and availability of equipment) at: less than 250 guilders 11%, 250 to 500 guilders 14%, 500 to 750 guilders 18%, 750 to 1000 guilders 8%, 1000 to 1250 guilders 18%, upwards of 1250 guilders 16%. A further 16% of the respondents had no opinion about the cost.

The services of the maternity home (nursing/care, hotel services, space) were estimated to have cost: less than 200 guilders 17%, 200

59

to 400 guilders 14 %, 400 to 600 guilders 40 %, upwards of 600 guilders 14 %. A further 14 % had no opinion.

Extra help
Since the cost of extra help is not covered by ziekenfonds or by insurance, this must, in principle, be born entirely by the patient herself. Therefore the estimated costs submitted by the respondents are probably the same as the actual costs paid by them.

The cost of extra help in the case of domiciliary delivery was estimated at: no extra costs 84 %, less than 75 guilders 4 %, 75 to 150 guilders 3 %, more than 150 guilders 3 %. –.7 % of the women had no idea of the cost.

Of the 35 women who had been delivered in a maternity home, 32 said that there had been no question of expenses for extra help. 3 women had no opinion.

The cost of extra domestic help during a hospital delivery were estimated at: no costs 74 %, less than 75 guilders 1 %, 75 to 150 guilders 1 %, more than 150 guilders 4 %, 20 % of the women had no opinion.

Cost of extra nourishment
For a domiciliary delivery the cost of extra nourishment was estimated at: no costs 65 %, less than 50 guilders 9 %, 50 to 100 guilders 6 %, 100 to 150 guilders 3 %, 150 to 200 guilders 3 %, 13 % had no opinion.

Of the 35 women who had been delivered in a maternity home 26 said there was no question of extra costs for food, 8 women had no opinion, and 1 estimated the cost of extra nourishment at less than 25 guilders.

Of those delivered in hospital, 79 % said there were no extra costs, 17 % had no opinion, 2 % estimated the cost at less than 25 guilders, 1 % estimated them at 75 to 150 guilders.

Other additional costs
For domiciliary deliveries: no additional costs 25 %, less than 75 guilders 25 %, 75 to 150 guilders 13 %, 150 to 225 guilders 12 %, upwards of 225 guilders 6 %, no opinion 19 %.

For delivery in a maternity home: no additional costs 49 %, less than 75 guilders 14 %, 150 to 225 guilders 3 %, upwards of 225 guilders 3 %, no opinion 31 %.

For a hospital delivery: no additional costs 44 %, less than 75 guilders 11 %, 75 to 150 guilders 6 %, 150 to 225 guilders 7 %, upwards of

60

225 guilders 7%, no opinion 26%.

Costs not covered by ziekenfonds or insurance
The women were asked how much they themselves had eventually had
to pay for the maternity services provided. Distinction has been made
between deliveries at home, in maternity homes and in hospitals.

*Table 40. Costs connected with delivery not covered by ziekenfonds
or insurance (in percentages)*

	Home	Maternity home	Hospital
All costs covered by insurance/ziekenfonds	2	–	46
Less than 250 guilders paid by patient herself	62	66	33
250 to 500 gulders paid by patient herself	18	20	8
500 to 1000 guilders paid by patient herself	13	9	3
Upwards of 1000 guilders paid by patient herself	4	6	4
Not known	1	–	6
Total number	238	35	124

In the case of nearly half the women delivered in hospital all the costs
were covered by ziekenfonds or insurance. For 2% of those delivered
at home this was not so.

6. SOME MEDICAL ASPECTS

Medical problems during delivery
The presence or absence of medical problems during delivery was
distributed over all four research areas as follows:

Table 41. Medical problems during delivery

	Total group	Utrecht	Tilburg	Rural area Utrecht	Rural area Tilburg
No problems	79	80	83	73	78
Problems that had been anticipated	8	9	10	7	5
Problems that had not been anticipated	12	10	7	19	12
Not known	2	1	–	1	5
Total number	400	100	100	100	100

In the case of 12% of the respondents medical problems had arisen which had not been foreseen. The number of times that unforeseen problems occurred was relatively high in the rural area of Utrecht and relatively low in Tilburg.

A comparison between town and country shows that there were more respondents in the towns whose deliveries presented no problems or whose problems were anticipated. In the country there were more women than in the towns whose problems had not been anticipated.

Difficulties with the newly-born infant

Table 42. Difficulties with the newly-born infant (in percentages)

Not known	Immediately after birth	In first 2 days	Later	No diffi- culties	Total number
1	11	4	4	81	400

The percentage of deliveries whereby difficulties presented themselves within the first 2 days was 15 including those which occurred directly after birth.

The respondents' answers showed that difficulties with the baby were: respiratory difficulties 13×, feeding problems 8×, wrong temperature 7×, need for incubation (especially with premature babies) 6×, physical abnormalities 7× (rupture, broken arm, etc.) infection 4×, jaundice 4×, intestinal troubles 2×, anaemia 2×, other 3×.

Baby's reaction to transfer home
In 25 of the cases where delivery took place in hospital or maternity home, the mother noticed a reaction in the baby on returning home. These were as follows:
a. negative: cried more 11×, restless, irritable 'not her usual self' 4×, caught a cold 3×, awake at night at different intervals than in hospital 2×, feeding problems 2×, not specified 1×;
b. positive: cried less 4×, slept better 1×, fed better 1×.

Infections directly after delivery
Distinction has been made between infections affecting the mother and those affecting the baby. Further distinction has been made according to the place where delivery occurred.

Table 43. Infection affecting the mother (in percentages)

	No infection	Infection	Total number
Home	94	6	238
Maternity home	94	6	35
Hospital	88	12	124

The percentage of infections was twice as high with hospital deliveries as with domiciliary deliveries.

A total of 31 respondents said that there had been some kind of infection following delivery (14 after domiciliary delivery, 2 after delivery in a maternity home, 15 after hospital delivery). In Utrecht there were 9 cases of infection (1 following domiciliary delivery, and 8 following hospital delivery); in Tilburg there were also 9 (2 following domiciliary delivery, 2 following delivery in a maternity home, 5 following hospital delivery); in the rural areas of Utrecht there were 6 cases (5 domiciliary, 1 hospital); in the rural areas of Tilburg there were 7 cases (6 domiciliary, 1 hospital). The domiciliary deliveries whereby maternal infection occurred were mostly in the rural areas (11 out of 14. There were 148 domiciliary deliveries in the rural areas as against 90 in the urban areas).

Infection occurred in 11 of the 165 deliveries managed by a family doctor, in 6 of the 107 managed by a midwife and in 12 of the 97 managed by a specialist.

The infections mentioned were localised as follows: breast $10 \times$; womb $4 \times$; vulva $2 \times$; sutures $2 \times$; ovaries $1 \times$; abdomen $1 \times$; labiae $1 \times$; bladder $4 \times$; leg $1 \times$; throat $1 \times$; not specified $4 \times$.

Maternal infections were treated by: a family doctor $17 \times$; specialist $10 \times$; midwife $1 \times$; nurse $1 \times$; some other person $4 \times$; not treated at all $1 \times$.

Table 44. Infant infection (in percentages)

	No infection	Infection	Total number
Home	98	2	238
Maternity home	94	6	35
Hospital	94	7	124

The percentage of infections was more than twice as high with hospital deliveries as with domiciliary deliveries. The absolute figures were too small to draw conclusions but there is a striking parallellism with the data on maternal infection. It should be remembered however, that there were far fewer abnormal cases delivered at home.

A total of 16 babies had contracted an infection: 6 out of 238 delivered at home, 2 out of 35 delivered in a maternity home and 8 out of 124 delivered in hospital. In Utrecht there were 8 cases of infection (2 after domiciliary delivery, 1 after delivery in a maternity home and 4 after hospital delivery); in Tilburg there were 3 cases (1 after delivery in a maternity home, 2 after hospital delivery), in the rural area of Utrecht there were 3 cases (2 after domiciliary delivery, 1 after hospital delivery). In the rural area of Tilburg there were also 3 cases (2 after domiciliary delivery, 1 after hospital delivery).

Infant infection occurred in 6 of the 165 deliveries managed by a family doctor, in 2 of the 107 managed by a midwife and in 4 of the 97 managed by a specialist.

The infections were as follows: boils 1×, skin infection 2×, navel infection 1×, vesicles 2×, diarrhea 2×, common cold 2×, not specified 3×.

The infections were treated by: family doctor 7×, specialist 5×, the mother herself 2×, some other person 2×.

Mental attitude to the delivery
Almost 1 woman in 4 had found her delivery an unpleasant experience (24%). The percentage was about the same with deliveries by family doctors and by midwives (18 and 19 respectively). With specialist deliveries the percentage was considerably higher (42%).

Reasons for dissatisfaction were as follows: (too) long duration of delivery 40×, appearance of medical complications 24×, pain 19×, 'difficult' 'trying' delivery 8×, worse than had been expected 7×, overdue 4×, fear 2×, unsatisfactory management of delivery 2×, not mentally prepared 1×, not specified 3×.

The investigation revealed 2 cases, both of them domiciliary, whereby no obstetrical assistance was available at the time of delivery.

4. Hospital deliveries according to information supplied by the Council for Medical Registration

The information supplied by the Council for Medical Registration concerns management of delivery, way in which patients were insured, indications on admission, husband's occupation (or that of the woman herself), age, parity (primi or multi) and average length of stay. The following tables refer to the clinical deliveries that took place in the years 1966 to 1970 in hospitals affiliated to the council for Medical Registration. In that period the number of births registered rose from a good 17,000 to almost 54,000. This increase is mainly the result of greater participation in the registration. More and more hospitals became involved so that in 1970 almost 60% of all clinical deliveries in Dutch hospitals were registered.

1. MANAGEMENT OF HOSPITAL DELIVERIES

Table 45. Management of deliveries (in percentages)

	1966	1967	1968	1969	1970
Obstetrician/Gynaecologist	80.8	81.2	84.1	82.2	80.1
Family doctor	13.6	11.8	9.5	8.5	8.6
Other doctor	0.4	0.3	0.3	0.2	0.4
Midwife	5.2	6.7	6.1	9.1	10.9
Total number	17,113	24,380	34,545	46,142	53,938

Four out of every five hospital deliveries were managed by a specialist. After 1968 the percentage of deliveries managed by a specialist decreased each year by 2%. The family doctor's share dropped from 13.6% in 1966 to only 8.6% in 1970. The midwife's share increased from 5.2% to 10.9%. Only a very small number of deliveries were managed by 'another doctor'.

The distribution of deliveries between family doctor, specialist and midwife varied with the size of the hospital.

65

Table 46. Size of hospital and management of deliveries (in percentages)

	Fewer than 125 beds	125 to 249 beds	250 to 374 beds	375 to 499 beds	500 and more beds
Specialist	77.4	76.7	74.3	88.4	96.4
Family doctor	21.0	12.9	14.7	7.7	2.9
Other doctor	–.–	0.7	0.4	0.8	0.1
Midwife	1.6	9.7	10.6	3.9	0.6
Total number	234	7,351	10,620	5,592	10,739

The midwife had a relatively large market share in the hospitals with 250 to 374 beds and those with 125 to 249 beds. Her share was small in the smallest and the largest hospitals.

The percentage share of the specialist was relatively small in the small to medium-sized hospitals and large in the larger hospitals. The doctor's share was relatively large in the small to medium-sized hospitals.

There is a striking difference in the management of hospital deliveries according to the way the patient was insured.

Table 47. Management of delivery of women insured with a ziekenfonds (in percentages)

	1966	1967	1968	1969	1970
Specialist	95.0	93.6	92.5	90.7	87.3
Family doctor	3.2	2.8	3.0	2.8	3.3
Other doctor	0.1	0.1	0.1	0.1	0.4
Midwife	1.7	3.5	4.4	6.4	9.0
Total number	10,235	15,558	22,886	30,141	36,182

Table 48. Management of delivery of privately insured women (in percentages)

	1966	1967	1968	1969	1970
Specialist	59.3	59.0	62.0	61.8	63.0
Family doctor	29.4	28.0	26.2	21.9	20.9
Other doctor	0.9	0.8	0.8	0.5	0.4
Midwife	10.5	12.2	11.0	15.8	15.7
Total number	6,697	8,594	9,874	13,850	16,243

About 90 % of the clinical deliveries of women insured with a ziekenfonds were managed by a specialist as against 60 % of those privately insured. The market share of the specialist in deliveries insured by ziekenfonds decreased (from 95 % in 1966 to 87.3 % in 1970).

In privately-insured deliveries it increased slightly (from 59.3 % in 1966 to 63 % in 1970).

The family doctor's market share of ziekenfonds-insured deliveries was small, about 3 %. The percentage remained about the same through the years. The family doctor's market share in privately-insured deliveries was relatively large. It dropped from 29.4 % in 1966 to 20.9 % in 1970.

The midwife's market share increased over the years especially in the case of ziekenfonds-insured deliveries. (1.7 % in 1966, 9 % in 1970) For privately-insured deliveries it increased from 10.5 % in 1966 to 15.7 % in 1970.

The following tables show the way the patients were insured in the case of clinical deliveries managed by a specialist, a family doctor and a midwife.

Table 49. Delivery managed by a specialist (in percentages)

	1966	1967	1968	1969	1970
Privately-insured	28.7	25.6	21.1	22.6	23.7
Ziekenfonds	70.4	73.6	73.0	72.0	73.0
Other and unknown	0.9	0.9	5.9	5.4	3.3
Total number	13,824	19,806	29,022	37,944	43,257

A good 70 % of the deliveries managed by a specialist concerned ziekenfonds-insured women. This percentage remained about the same from 1966 to 1970.

Table 50. Deliveries managed by a family doctor (in percentages)

	1966	1967	1968	1969	1970
Privately-insured	84.7	84.1	78.5	77.6	73.5
Ziekenfonds	14.2	15.2	21.0	21.7	26.2
Other and unknown	1.1	0.7	0.5	0.7	0.3
Total number	2,330	2,868	3,298	3,904	4,615

About three quarters of the hospital deliveries managed by a family doctor concerned privately-insured women. The percentage of his share decreased in the case of privately-insured and increased in the case of ziekenfonds-insured women.

67

Table 51. Delivery managed by a midwife (in percentages)

	1966	1967	1968	1969	1970
Privately-insured	78.1	64.4	51.4	52.4	54.5
Ziekenfonds	19.0	33.1	47.0	45.8	55.7
Other and unknown	2.1	2.3	1.6	1.8	0.8
Total number	896	1,628	2,124	4,197	5,860

There was a noticeable decrease in the share percentage of privately-insured women in hospital deliveries managed by a midwife and a noticeable increase in the share of ziekenfonds-insured women.

The Council for Medical Registration makes a distinction between deliveries without medical indication, deliveries with medical indicaton and deliveries whereby there was urgency indication during labour. These were distributed amongst the clinical deliveries as follows:

Table 52. Indication for clinical delivery (in percentages)

	1966	1967	1968	1969	1970
No medical indication	31.5	27.0	28.9	31.8	30.6
Urgency indication during labour	20.7	21.7	17.9	18.4	16.1
Medical indication	47.8	51.3	53.2	49.8	53.3
Total number	17,113	24,380	34,545	46,142	53,938

In these particular years, about 30 % of the clinical deliveries were not medically indicated. There was a noticeable number of urgency indications: 1 out of every 5 or 6 clinical deliveries were in this category. In spite of a probable more liberal use of medical indication, the percentage of urgency indications dropped only slightly.

About half of the hospital deliveries came under the heading – Delivery with medical indication. There were noticeable differences in the percentage distribution of management of delivery according to category of indication.

Table 53. Management of hospital deliveries without medical indication (in percentages)

	1966	1967	1968	1969	1970
Specialist	45.4	39.3	49.8	47.4	39.3
Family doctor	39.1	38.6	30.2	25.0	26.1
Other doctor	1.0	0.9	0.9	0.5	0.9
Midwife	14.5	21.2	19.1	27.1	33.7
Total number	5,385	6,582	9,975	14,685	16,498

68

More than half of the hospital deliveries without medical indication were managed by a family doctor or a midwife. The specialist's share varied between 39 % and 50 % and evidenced fairly strong fluctuations. The family doctor's share decreased constantly (except for a small increase in 1970) and the midwife's share increased; in 1970 it was twice what it was in 1966.

Table 54. Management of delivery with urgency indication during labour (in percentages)

	1966	1967	1968	1969	1970
Specialist	97.8	98.6	99.2	99.0	98.6
Family doctor	1.4	0.8	0.6	0.5	0.4
Other doctor	0.1	–.–	–.–	–.–	0.1
Midwife	0.7	0.6	0.2	0.5	0.9
Total number	3,536	5,299	6,195	8,480	8,681

Table 55. Management of delivery with medical indication (in percentages)

	1966	1967	1968	1969	1970
Specialist	96.8	96.0	97.5	98.3	98.0
Family doctor	2.1	2.3	1.3	0.8	1.0
Other doctor	–.–	0.1	0.1	0.1	0.2
Midwife	1.1	1.6	1.1	0.8	0.8
Total number	8,192	12,499	18,375	22,977	28,759

Almost all the deliveries with urgency indication or medical indication were managed by a specialist. The share of the family doctor and the midwife in these cases was insignificant.

2. INDICATION FOR CLINICAL DELIVERY

There was found to be a connection between the insurance category of the patient and the indication for clinical delivery.

Table 56.

	1966 Zieken- fonds	1967 Zieken- fonds	1968 Zieken- fonds	1969 Zieken- fonds	1970 Zieken- fonds
Without medical indication	15.7	14.4	18.4	20.6	21.9
Urgency indication	26.8	27.1	21.4	22.4	19.0
Medical indication	57.5	58.6	60.2	57.1	59.1
Total number	10,235	15,558	22,886	30,141	36,182

	1966 Private	1967 Private	1968 Private	1969 Private	1970 Private
Without medical indication	55.3	49.8	45.1	49.1	47.1
Urgency indication	11.4	12.1	12.6	11.8	10.4
Medical indication	33.3	38.1	42.3	39.1	42.5
Total number	6,697	8,594	9,874	13,850	16,243

The numbers of privately-insured women who arranged to be delivered in hospital without medical indication were considerably greater than of ziekenfonds-insured women. The percentage of urgency indications during labour was considerably lower in the case of privately-insured women than of ziekenfonds-insured women. The percentage of hospital deliveries without medical indication amongst ziekenfonds-insured women increased from 14.4 in 1967 to 21.9. The percentage amongst privately-insured women fluctuated between 45 and 50 in the years 1967 to 1970.

The percentage of deliveries with medical indication amongst privately-insured women increased from 33.3 to 42.5. Amongst ziekenfonds-insured women it fluctuated between 55 and 60.

The question was examined as to whether there was a connection between the occupational groups defined by the Council for Medical Registration and indications for admission to hospital. Since occupation was related to insurance category and this latter to the medical indication a distinction was made in the analysis, between ziekenfonds-insured and private-insured women.

In general, there were considerable differences between the ziekenfonds-insured women and the privately-insured women in the different occupational groups. Within the separate groups, the percentage of hospital deliveries without medical indication was always considerably higher amongst privately-insured women than amongst ziekenfonds-insured women. A connection between occupational group and indication should mean that in one particular group of either ziekenfonds- or

70

privately-insured women there would be relatively low or high percentages of, for instance, hospital deliveries without medical indication. However, in most groups there were fairly big fluctuations.

The following tables show the occupational groups of both privately-insured and hospital-insured women (separately) in which the highest percentages of hospital deliveries without medical indications were registered.

Table 57. Indication for clinical delivery of ziekenfonds-insured women according to occupational grouping (in percentages), 1970

	Farmers (owners or managers)	Farm workers	Clerical workers	Professionally employed
Without medical indication	6.7	9.7	25.4	30.3
Urgency indication during labour	24.6	22.8	17.3	17.1
Medical indication	68.7	67.5	57.3	52.6
Total number	525	487	10.558	152

Amongst ziekenfonds-insured women, the highest percentage of hospital deliveries without medical indication was found in the categories of professionally employed and clerical workers. The percentage was low amongst farmers and farm workers.

Table 58. Indication for clinical delivery of privately-insured women according to occupational grouping (in percentages), 1970

	Farmer (owners and managers)	Professionally employed	Manual workers
Without medical indication	18.0	48.6	66.3
Urgency indication during labour	20.9	9.6	41.8
Medical indication	61.1	41.8	25.8
Total number	716	1,246	1,793

Amongst privately-insured women, there were high percentages of hospital deliveries without medical indication in the categories of manual workers and of the professionally employed. Percentages were low in the category of farmers and farm managers.

71

Only in the categories of farmers and of professionally employed was the picture stable.

Both amongst the ziekenfonds-insured and the privately-insured there were relatively low percentages of hospital deliveries without medical indication in the categories of farmers and farm managers. The percentages were relatively high in the categories of professionally employed.

There was a connection between the patient's age and the indication for clinical delivery.

Table 59. Indication for clinical delivery according to age (in percentages), 1970

	15-19 years	20-24 years	25-29 years	30-34 years	35-39 years	40 years and older
Without medical indication	40.9	36.0	30.8	25.9	18.9	13.6
Urgent indication during labour	17.2	18.6	15.3	13.8	14.5	12.9
With medical indication	41.9	45.4	53.9	60.2	66.6	73.5
Total number	3,250	17,343	17,410	9,431	4,647	1,843

The category of no medical indication decreased as the age of the women increased. On the other hand, the category with medical indication increased in each successive age-group. This also applied to the other 4 years concerned in the investigation.

The question was examined as to whether there was any connection between the decision to be delivered in hospital without medical indication and the parity of the patient (as between primi and multi), considering also the link between age and parity (see table 60).

According to table 60 the percentage of deliveries without medical indication was slightly higher amongst primiparae under 25 years of age than amongst multiparae in the same age-group. After the age of 25, the percentage of deliveries without medical indication was slightly higher amongst multiparae than amongst primiparae. The percentage of clinical deliveries without medical indication amongst primiparae over 40 years of age dropped from 26.6 in 1966 to 6.3 in 1970. There were noticeable differences in the percentages of indication for clinical delivery from one province to another. The following table shows these differences in respect of both privately-insured and ziekenfonds-insured patients.

72

Table 60. Admission to hospital without medical indication related to age and parity (in percentages)

	15-19 years		20-24 years		25-29 years	
	Primi	Multi	Primi	Multi	Primi	Multi
1966	36.8	31.9	36.9	32.6	31.1	32.1
1967	36.7	27.8	31.9	30.3	26.2	28.9
1968	42.5	43.8	34.6	33.5	27.6	29.1
1969	43.4	37.7	37.6	37.8	29.1	32.3
1970	41.3	37.6	36.4	35.1	30.1	31.2
	30-34 years		35-39 years		40 years and older	
	Primi	Multi	Primi	Multi	Primi	Multi
1966	29.7	32.3	26.2	25.0	26.6	22.8
1967	23.0	25.7	16.3	20.5	15.4	15.3
1968	22.2	24.3	14.5	20.3	9.9	16.8
1969	24.2	28.1	17.6	20.6	7.8	18.2
1970	22.9	26.8	13.2	20.0	6.3	14.7

Percentage of primiparae minus percentage of multiparae

1966	4.9	4.3	−1	−1.6	1.2	3.8
1967	8.9	1.6	−2.7	−2.7	−4.2	0.1
1968	−1.3	1.1	−1.5	−2.1	−5.8	−6.9
1969	5.7	−0.2	−3.3	−3.9	−3	−10.4
1970	3.7	1.3	−1.1	−3.9	−6.8	−8.4

In Noord-Holland, Groningen, Overijssel, Utrecht and Zuid-Holland there were relatively high percentages of clinical delieveries without medical indication amongst ziekenfonds-insured women. (25 % and more). The percentages were low in Noord-Brabant, Friesland, Drente, Gelderland and Limburg (less than 10 %) (see table 61, page 74).

The difference between the province with the highest percentage of clinical deliveries without medical indication amongst ziekenfonds-insured women, Noord-Holland, and that with the lowest, Noord-Brabant, was 40 %.

Provinces with a high percentage of clinical deliveries without medical indication amongst privately-insured women were Friesland, Groningen, Noord-Holland and Zuid-Holland (60 % and more); provinces with a low percentage were Limburg, Noord-Brabant, Overijssel and Drente (less than 30 %).

The difference between the province with the highest percentage of clinical deliveries without medical indication amongst privately-insured women, Friesland, and that with the lowest percentage, Limburg, was 63.5 %.

Table 61. Indication for clinical delivery per province in respect of ziekenfonds-insured and privately-insured patients (in percentages) 1970*

| | Ziekenfonds-insured | | | |
	Without medical indication	Urgent indication	Medical indication	Total number
Groningen	27.6	13.1	59.3	1642
Friesland	3.8	32.8	63.4	1024
Drente	4.9	27.8	67.3	990
Overijssel	27.6	22.9	49.5	4211
Gelderland	8.8	24.4	66.8	3868
Utrecht	27.0	17.0	56.0	2348
Noord-Holland	43.1	12.2	44.6	5711
Zuid-Holland	25.0	17.7	57.2	7364
Noord-Brabant	3.0	28.3	68.7	3907
Limburg	9.5	12.7	77.9	4244

| | Privately-insured | | | |
	Without medical indication	Urgent indication	Medical indication	Total number
Groningen	58.0	10.4	31.6	1187
Friesland	72.4	4.8	22.8	479
Drente	29.3	22.8	48.0	246
Overijssel	26.4	18.4	55.2	875
Gelderland	34.9	15.0	50.1	1184
Utrecht	39.6	11.5	48.9	1002
Noord-Holland	60.7	7.0	32.3	6327
Zuid-Holland	59.9	7.2	32.9	4599
Noord-Brabant	27.9	17.7	54.4	1731
Limburg	8.9	9.5	81.6	1234

* Because of the small number of clinical deliveries registered in Zeeland, this province was omitted from the investigation.

In general, the provinces where relatively the most hospital deliveries without medical indication took place, had the lowest percentages of urgency indications during labour. An exception to this was Limburg where there were relatively low percentages of hospital deliveries without medical indication as well as low percentages of urgency indications during labour.

The number of gynaecologists, family doctors and midwives per province in 1970 was as follows:

74

Table 62.   Number of gynaecologists, family doctors and midwives per province (1970). (source G.H.I.)

	Gynaecologists		Family doctors		Midwives	
	Absolute	Per 10,000	Absolute	Per 10,000	Absolute	Per 100,000
Groningen	14	0.3	191	3.7	27	4.8
Friesland	11	0.2	208	4.0	20	3.8
Drente	10	0.3	131	3.6	17	4.6
Overijssel	21	0.2	295	3.2	50	5.3
Gelderland	30	0.2	519	3.4	76	5.0
Utrecht	21	0.3	301	3.8	45	5.6
Noord-Holland	73	0.3	834	3.7	157	7.0
Zuid-Holland	85	0.3	1020	3.4	163	5.5
Zeeland	5	0.2	123	4.0	4	1.3
Noord-Brabant	37	0.2	553	3.1	106	5.9
Limburg	21	0.2	309	3.1	110	11.0
Total number	328	(0.3)	4484	(3.5)	775	(6.0)

Provinces with a relatively large number of gynaecologists (0.3 per 10,000 inhabitants) were Groningen, Drente, Utrecht, Noord-Holland and Zuid-Holland.

In Limburg there was a noticeably large number of midwives (11 per 100,000 inhabitants). In this province, as also in Noord-Brabant, there was a relatively small number of family doctors (3.1 per 10,000 inhabitants).

Table 63 shows quite clearly that the percentage of hospital deliveries without medical indication increased with the number of inhabitants; that of deliveries with medical indication decreased reciprocally.

In the years 1966 to 1969 too, the percentage of deliveries without medical indication was low in the districts with a small population and high in those with a large population.

Table 63. Indication for clinical delivery per size of district in respect of ziekenfonds-insured inhabitants and privately-insured inhabitants (in percentages) 1970

| | Ziekenfonds-insured | | | |
	Without medical indication	*Urgent indication*	*With medical indication*	*Total number*
Less than 5,000 inhabitants	11.9	22.6	65.5	2,594
5- 20,000 inhabitants	12.1	24.4	63.5	8,258
20- 50,000 inhabitants	16.0	19.6	64.3	5,769
50-100,000 inhabitants	24.7	19.4	55.9	5,874
100-500,000 inhabitants	26.0	17.2	56.8	7,763
500,000 and more	42.7	8.4	49.0	4,924

| | Privately-insured | | | |
	Without medical indication	*Urgent indication*	*With medical indication*	*Total number*
Less than 5,000 inhabitants	24.4	14.6	61.0	1,028
5- 20,000 inhabitants	35.9	13.4	50.7	4,036
20- 50,000 inhabitants	43.1	10.8	46.1	2,495
50-100,000 inhabitants	40.0	11.7	48.3	2,191
100-500,000 inhabitants	53.7	9.9	36.4	3,834
500,000 and above	72.7	3.7	23.7	2,659

3. AVERAGE LENGTH OF STAY

There were distinct differences in the average length of stay depending on who had managed the delivery. The average length of stay for delivery managed by a specialist is longer, doubtless because these are often pathological deliveries. Family doctors and midwives as a rule manage only deliveries whereby no unusual risk is expected. Insight into the differences in average length of stay between deliveries managed by specialists, family doctors and midwives was obtained by categorizing according to both management of delivery and indication. The following table shows the average length of stay for deliveries without medical indication.

76

Table 64. Average length of stay for hospital deliveries without medical indication (in days)

	1966	1967	1968	1969	1970
Specialist	11.2	10.2	9.7	10.5	9.8
Family doctor	8.8	8.7	8.5	8.2	7.5
Midwife	8.9	8.6	8.6	8.9	7.6

The average length of stay for deliveries managed by a specialist without medical indication was longer than for those managed by a family doctor or a midwife – a difference of 2 days in 1970. This longer stay was an additional factor besides the higher fee involved, that made a specialist-managed delivery more expensive. Deliveries without medical indication managed by a specialist as shown by table 65, involved a stay that was, on average, about 3 or 4 days shorter than those with medical indication managed by a specialist.

Table 65. Average length of stay for deliveries managed by a specialist (in days)

	1966	1967	1968	1969	1970
Without medical indication	11.2	10.2	9.7	10.5	9.8
Urgency indication	11.2	10.2	10.4	10.4	9.9
With medical indication	13.9	14.1	13.7	13.7	12.9

It is notable that there is little difference in the average length of stay between deliveries managed by a specialist without medical indication and those with urgency indication. The slight difference may, in part, be due to the fact that in cases of urgency there is no question of antenatal stay in hospital.

The question was examined as to whether any connection existed between the way the women were insured and the average length of stay. Since the indication is an important factor in determining the length of stay this has been accounted for in the table.

Table 66. Average length of stay in respect of indication and insurance (in days)

	1966 Zieken-fonds	1967 Zieken-fonds	1968 Zieken-fonds	1969 Zieken-fonds	1970 Zieken-fonds
Without medical indication	11.0	10.1	9.6	10.5	8.6
Urgency indication during labour	11.3	10.5	10.4	10.4	9.9
With medical indication	14.2	14.3	14.1	13.9	13.1
	Private	Private	Private	Private	Private
Without medical indication	9.4	8.8	8.6	8.6	8.2
Urgency indication during labour	10.8	10.7	10.4	10.2	9.6
With medical indication	12.6	12.9	12.5	12.9	12.1

In the case of clinical deliveries without medical indication, the average length of stay was shorter for privately-insured women than for those insured with a ziekenfonds. For the years 1966 to 1970 respectively 1,6; 1,3; 1,9; and 0,4 days.

In the case of clinical deliveries with medical indication, the average length of stay was also shorter for privately-insured women, respectively 2; 1.4; 1.6; 1; and 1 day.

If the conclusions drawn from table 31 – that privately-insured women are more often admitted to hospital with medical indication than those insured with a ziekenfonds, should be found to hold good on a wider scale, then there will be relatively more pathological cases amongst ziekenfonds-insured women than amongst those privately-insured. This could in part, explain the relatively shorter average stay for clinical delivery with medical indication of privately-insured women.

The average length of stay was found of women in the different occupational categories in respect of indication (see table 67).

The average length of stay was on the whole, longest in the categories of farmers and farm-workers; it was shortest in the category of independently employed. This applied both to deliveries without and those with medical indication.

There are two probable reasons for the higher average length of stay in the categories of farmers and farm-workers.

Both of these categories live in the country. The percentage of clinical

Table 67. *Average length of stay in respect of occupation and indication (in days)*

	1966			1967			1968			1969			1970		
	WMi	Ui	Mi	WMi	Ui	Mi	WMi	Ui	Mi	WMi	Ui	Mi	WMi	Ui	Mi
Farmers (owners, managers)	11.5	12.9	17.0	9.6	12.7	17.1	9.1	10.5	15.0	9.0	10.9	16.6	8.9	10.3	14.7
Other managerial functions	9.8	11.1	14.1	9.0	10.3	14.1	9.0	10.2	14.1	8.7	9.9	13.1	8.0	10.4	12.9
Independently employed	9.0	10.2	12.0	8.9	8.9	11.6	8.3	10.9	11.0	8.4	10.0	11.6	7.7	9.4	10.7
Other clerical and administrative workers	9.8	11.2	13.5	9.1	10.7	13.3	9.0	10.4	13.5	9.3	10.4	15.3	8.3	10.2	12.6
Farm workers	11.4	11.0	15.8	9.2	11.3	16.9	11.0	10.3	15.9	9.5	10.0	15.6	8.7	9.9	14.7
Other manual workers	10.1	11.1	14.5	9.6	10.7	14.3	9.4	10.5	14.0	9.3	10.3	13.9	8.3	10.0	13.3

deliveries is considerably lower in the country than in the towns. For this reason, clinical deliveries with medical indication will, in both groups, include a relatively large number of pathological cases.

Moreover, in rural areas, the distance to a hospital is generally greater than in urban areas. This might be a reason for allowing a wider margin between the expected time of delivery and the time of going into hospital.

No obvious connection could be found between the size of the institution and the average length of stay.

Table 68. Average length of stay related to size of hospital (1968)

	Fewer than 125 beds	125 to 249 beds	250 to 374 beds	375 to 499	500 and more beds
Average length of stay	12.7 days	11.6 days	11.6 days	12.9 days	11.5 days

5. Conclusion

Maternity services are suitable material for analysis in the framework of a market. The services can be individually demanded and supplied whilst the prices can also be charged individually. However, this is a market with somewhat remarkable characteristics, one of the most notable of these being the power of the suppliers. The doctors especially, by diagnosing indications requiring the use of particular services, are in this strong position of power. Over the years, the birth of a baby has come to be more and more a medical occurrence and the medical profession is largely responsible for this development. On the demand side it is notable that the consumer has little knowledge of the various alternatives available to her and has small chance of having her preferences put into effect. Moreover the market shows little transparency, partly because of the part of broker played by the insurer. The nature of the market makes it inevitable that the Government should exercise control over it.

It is often said that the number of women who prefer to be delivered in hospital is increasing. It is indeed a fact that the percentage of hospital deliveries is growing and that of domiciliary deliveries is declining. This only means, however, that the effective demand for hospital services has increased. It is very questionable whether the demand corresponds to actual preference. Substantiation of the demand for maternity arrangements depends on many factors, some of them coercive. Medical, economic, geographical and social considerations as well as some connected with insurance and other chance circumstances often have a great deal of influence. The element of choice is, in fact, frequently limited by these factors. One wonders whether the opportunity to make a choice is not even more restricted than it need be.

More than 1 in 4 of the respondents concerned in our enquiry had been admitted to hospital on medical indication. In such cases the use of hospital services and specialist attention seems unavoidable. Equally in the case of problem situations connected with family or domiciliary circumstances, admission to hospital or maternity home might be a near-necessity.

The high prices of certain maternity services (hospital, specialist) tend to put them beyond the reach of people belonging to lower income groups in cases where, in the absence of medical indication, a choice would be theoretically possible. Compulsorily insured women are restricted in their choice because, wherever possible, they have to use the services of a midwife in order to be re-imbursed for the costs involved. Freedom of choice might be limited by replacement of the person who was to have managed the delivery or by admission to a teaching hospital where the patient does not know who is to manage her delivery. Often, too, there is little freedom in the choice of a hospital.

The majority of the respondents concerned in the field research expressed a preference for delivery at home. There were more positive reactions with regard to the place where delivery took place from women who had been delivered at home than from those delivered in hospital. This was also the case in respect of the last delivery but one and the last delivery but two.

A positive attitude to domiciliary deliveries was further demonstrated by the fact that the respondents more frequently expressed a preference for delivery at home rather than in hospital. Moreover their opinions on a number of statements concerning the place of delivery showed that they were positively in favour of having their babies at home. Most of the women thought that a hospital delivery should continue to be an exception. It was not, either in their own opinion or that of their families, considered to be pleasanter than delivery at home.

On the strength of the above findings it may be concluded that many consumers attached great value to domiciliary delivery and preferred it to delivery elsewhere.

The circumstances under which a domiciliary delivery takes place (familiar surroundings, homeliness, being with the family) were generally preferred to those surrounding a hospital delivery. So it would be against the wishes of many consumers if the alternative of domiciliary delivery was no longer available. Domiciliary deliveries are, generally speaking, considerably cheaper than hospital deliveries. If hospitalization of pregnant women were to become a general practice, it would entail an extra cost of about 100 million guilders per year, based on prices of 1971.

It should be borne in mind that a higher percentage of hospital deliveries would mean a lower marginal output. Because increasingly more normal deliveries take place in hospital which could equally well, or almost as well have been carried out at home, the law of diminishing returns is going to play an important part in the issue. It seems therefore desirable both from an economic point of view and in order to meet the legitimate wishes of the consumer, for the possibility to remain open of maternity services being supplied in the patients' own homes.

It is important for the consumers of medical services to receive objective information since they are only to a limited degree in a position to judge what services they need and to assess the quality of those services. The suppliers, particularly the doctors, exercise a great deal of influence on the demand from consumers. Since the personal interest of the suppliers is here involved, the situation is a rather dubious one. One of the problems that make it difficult to give advisory information is that it is not possible to state in exact terms the difference in quality between the package of maternity services provided at home and that provided in hospital. As a result, the qualitative difference cannot be related to the difference in cost.

There are elements present in the different types of insurance that stimulate the trend towards hospital delivery. Ziekenfonds-insured women receive partial reimbursement for nursing/care in hospital even when there is no medical indication. As a rule, privately-insured women are not reimbursed for the cost of delivery and maternity care at home. So the privately-insured are financially better off with hospital delivery on medical indication.

In general, privately-insured women make more use of hospital maternity services than do ziekenfonds-insured women. There were clearly more deliveries with medical indication amongst the privately-insured than amongst the ziekenfonds-insured women, of the 400 concerned in the field inquiry. Of the privately-insured 31% were admitted to hospital on medical indication; of the ziekenfonds-insured the percentage was 21. It seems unlikely that the type of insurance should have any influence on the frequency of 'at risk' situations amongst pregnant women. From the data supplied by the Council for Medical Registration it can be deduced that the demand for different kinds of services was connected with the type of insurance. There were more privately-insured women than ziekenfonds-insured women who bought maternity services to be supplied in hospital without there being any question of medical indication. Almost half of the clinical deliveries

83

amongst privately-insured were without medical indication as against 1 in 5 deliveries amongst the ziekenfonds-insured. The management of clinical deliveries seemed also to be connected with the way the patient was insured. About three quarters of the deliveries managed by specialists were of ziekenfonds-insured women. Three quarters of those managed by family doctors were of privately-insured women.

If the Dutch system of maternity welfare is to be maintained, the work situation of both family doctors and midwives will have to be such as to enable them to continue to carry out domiciliary deliveries. Attending deliveries entails irregular pressure on a doctor's practice, i.e. disutility. Moreover it hinders him in other branches of his work and in the exploitation of other sources of income. The fee that he receives for maternity services is perhaps too low in relation to the disutility and to the relative returns that result from applying his potentialities in other directions.

Midwives seem increasingly inclined to attach themselves to hospitals with the result that there is a shortage of midwives to manage domiciliary deliveries.

The rights and working conditions of the independently employed midwife have a lot do to with this. However, in order to carry out her duties in the patients' home, it it not essential for the midwife to have her own private practice. She could still supervise domiciliary deliveries if she were employed by some organization. Both family doctors and midwives are very much dependent on the availability of certain additional, complementary services that complete the package (viz. maternity helps).

The (obstetrical) specialists have great influence on the insight into the relative risks that accompany deliveries at home and in hospital. This gives them a very considerable grip on the market. Not only does their opinion carry a lot of weight with the customers for maternity services, but they can also be sure that other suppliers (family doctors and midwives) will also be attentive to what they say. Moreover, they exercise control over the introduction of new specialists so that the volume of the supply side of the market is largely determined by them.

The different packages of maternity services demanded can very considerably. Since they are adapted to individual requirements they can be called heterogeneous.

The market is intransparent. The consumer is only partly in a position to decide for herself what services she needs. She does not generally know of all the alternatives available to her. If she does know of some of them, it is still very difficult for her to assess their quality. Her insight into prices is limited, largely owing to the system of insurance that results in ill-definement of costs and prices. The suppliers of basic maternity services have an individual relationship with the customers for maternity services. The question may be asked whether the suppliers are always sufficiently aware of the consumers' wishes. There are several areas where family doctors and midwives are supplying fewer and fewer maternity services in the patients' homes in spite of the wishes of an important section of these consumers.

Another aspect of the market's intransparency is the lack of sufficient pre-information for the supplier as to the time at which maternity assistance has to be supplied. That this exact time is not easy to foresee is apparent from the number of hospital admissions with urgency indication during labour.

Divisibility of production factors is important for any possible adjustment to a changed market situation. A doctor may be regarded as a production unit with a certain amount of flexibility in respect of services to be supplied.

This applies more to the family doctor, whose services in the field of maternity work constitute only a part of his total package of services than it does to the midwife. This latter has specialized in one single production category and her income depends on the services she supplies in this field. In order to assure herself of a reasonable livelihood she has to attain a certain turnover of maternity services. Curtailment of production means loss of skill in supplying high-quality maternity services if production falls below a certain minimum. In other words, insufficient use of productive capacity causes accelerated 'wear'. In reverse, there is another equally important situation, namely, that within certain limits, frequent use of productive capacity results from a qualitative point of view, to a higher productive capacity.

In the short run the size of a hospital maternity unit is a given factor. There is a relatively narrow margin wherein production may be curtailed or expanded. A 90 % occupancy of hospital capacity is the standard for determining rates in accordance with the recommendations of the Central Office for Hospital Tariffs. Occupancy of less than 90 % in any particular unit, unless compensated by above-average percentages of occupancy in other units, results in exploitation losses. Here the diversity factor is important. It is necessary to maintain some over-capacity in order to fulfill the availability function. It is not in the interests of the hospital to curtail the production of maternity services for reasons of market policy. In the face of the demand for hospital maternity service on grounds of medical indication, a curtailment for reasons of market policy would also be unacceptable from a social point of view. Production can be increased in the short run only within the limits of productive capacity (number of beds, staffing). It is, however, possible to alter the production structure by, for instance, manipulating the duration of the stay.

In conclusion it can be said that the volume of production can generally be adjusted only within certain limits.

The demand for maternity services reaches a peak in Spring. If this fact, together with the limited divisibility of production factors, gives rise to over-capacity during the rest of the year, the result will be an increase in cost prices.

The market for maternity services does not stand alone but is part of the market for health services in general. These are an integral part of the present-day welfare society within the economic and social order that exists at this time. Before a woman becomes pregnant, maternity services are, as far as she is concerned, in a state of competition with other products. This fact is obscured because of a decision having to be taken regarding a demand for services that are to be supplied nine months later. The 'pill' and other contraceptives help the consumer to put into effect her preference for products other than maternity services. When pregnancy occurs it leads automatically, as it were, to a demand for maternity services which is only limited by interruption of the pregnancy whether deliberate or accidental. This demand cannot be postponed until a time that is financially more convenient for the consumer. Nature takes no account of economic considerations. Price is not the only decisive factor, and it is hardly ever the most important one, in the decision to buy particular maternity services. When pregnancy is concerned, there is not so much a question of competition against the demand for other products or services but of competition amongst themselves between the different maternity services. If the consumer has a choice of alternative services and if substitution between maternity services is possible, then price factors may be of importance to demand.

In general there is little flexibility with regard to entering or leaving the market for health services and the subsidiary market for maternity services. The supplier's entry is subject to a number of regulations

86

(licences, approvals, dependence on subsidies) many of which are legally foundations. Free entry is also restricted by training requirements and training opportunities. Changes in supply capacity do not usually take place overnight. As a rule, the process takes some time.

The market for maternity services is characterized by a large degree of intransparency, the services are heterogeneous and there is some personal preference, productive capacity can adjust itself in the short run to only a limited degree, and in the long run only slowly, and the suppliers' entry into the market is restricted by a great many regulations. Therefore the market can be typified as 'imperfect' with a closed character.

Analysis of the market type is further based on the number of participants. Since supply and demand of maternity services are only relevant within a limited geographical area, there would be a market type with oligopoly on the supply side and oligopsony on the demand side, if quantity alone were the criterium.

In the case of oligopoly the turnover of one particular supplier is influenced by price activity on the part of other suppliers, unless he adjusts his own prices to the situation. One of the characteristics of oligopoly is the fact that the behaviour of one supplier is influenced by a certain kind of behaviour on the part of other suppliers. In the market for maternity services this kind of manipulation is completely absent. In this market it is not usual to try to increase turnover by means of price manipulation. A situation that can be observed from time to time whereby maternity services are offered by hospitals at dump prices (below cost price) is an example of an attempt to increase turnover by means of price mechanism.

However this is exceptional. A hospital might resort to dumping in order to achieve more complete occupancy of the maternity unit or so that sufficient deliveries can be carried out to fulfill the training requirements of nursing staff. Because of the peak period, a hospital has to provide a relatively large amount of accommodation in the maternity unit. This results in an average low level of occupancy not only with regard to space but also to the staff who cannot easily be employed in other units.

Neither is there on the demand side of the market, at least at micro level, any influencing of prices by the action of individual buyers. It is indeed true that on the demand side of the market, individual buyers are influenced by the behaviour of other buyers, but this influence is not concerned with prices. Individual buyers are far more likely to be

87

faced with fixed prices on which they can exercise no influence. The prices are a given factor. As in the case of polyopsony, buyers in this market have to do with prices which for them are a datum.

Monopoly elements are clearly present in the market for maternity services. There are various causal factors for the occurrence of monopoly. In respect of maternity services, monopoly by big production unit and the cartel are relevant aspects of legal monopoly.

Knowledge and skill can also give rise to monopoly. A significant example of measures designed to preserve such a monopoly is the 18th century case of the 'forceps secret' (a method of using certain kinds of forceps for difficult deliveries) which was handed down from father to son. A monopoly situation arises when a seller has practically no competition to fear because he is the sole supplier of certain services.

In rural districts this situation often occurs in respect of maternity services. The hospital and the specialist employed there are monopolists if there is only one hospital in the district and domiciliary delivery is out of the question because of a medical indication.

When two or more hospital or maternity centres are run by different confessional groups, each hospital or centre supplies its own variety of services as it were and this results in a (limited) monopoly situation. Naturally, this is only true if the consumer attaches some value to such heterogenity.

In a monopoly situation, a single supplier (individual monopoly) or a group of suppliers (collective monopoly or cartel) can determine the price more or less independently. It is necessary when considering the question as to how important monopoly aspects are to the market for maternity services, to make distinction between determination of prices for ziekenfonds-insured buyers and that of prices for the privately-insured. With regard to the ziekenfonds-insured buyers, negotiations take place between the organizations of suppliers (family doctors, midwives, specialists) and representatives of the buyers (collective ziekenfonds organizations) acting as brokers. So the price is not in this case, independently determined. Nevertheless, it is true that powerful collective action of the suppliers places them in a very powerful position and their influence on price determination is considerable. Family doctors, midwives and specialists have much more freedom in the determination of prices to be charged to patients not insured by a ziekenfonds. Price agreements between associations of sellers and buyers are here far less customary. The supply side of the market draws up (unilateral) recommendations which are used as a basis on which to determine prices. Examples of such recommendations are those relating to family doctors' and specialists' fees. Particularly in the case of specialists there are considerable differences between the prices of services to ziekenfonds-insured patients and those of services to privately-insured patients. The price charged for a gynaecologist's services to privately-insured patients in class 2A is about 5 times as much as that charged to ziekenfonds patients, (insured in class III). This state of affairs can be regarded as a form of price-discrimination or price-differentiation. Some of the differences in the price charged to the consumer can be only partially related back to difference in cost. On the part of the supplier income motives are a matter of consideration. By their behaviour they bring about a concrete example of income redistribution between ziekenfonds-insured and privately-insured patients. The suppliers recognize on the demand side two quite distinct markets – one concerning ziekenfonds patients and the other for the privately insured. On the one market the suppliers operate with higher prices than on the other. The markets are separated from each other by law whilst the nature of the merchandise precludes resale from the low-priced market to the high-priced market. Because of this, the differences in price can be maintained. Moreover, there is differentiation regarding prices charged to the different insurance classes.

The prices for hospital nursing and care determined by the maternity centres are based on cost price – a criterium which gives rise to different selling prices. Price manipulation is, in principle, precluded by the offer of services on the basis of cost price.

The fact that prices for hospital services are determined in accordance with the recommendations of the Central Office for Hospital Tariffs places the hospitals in a somewhat enhanced position in respect of competition with alternative services. Since hospitals are not permitted to calculate depreciation on the basis of replacement value and to allow for interest on their own invested capital, the tariff is in fact too low. The recommendations of the Central Office for Hospital Tariffs do not apply to teaching hospitals which means that these can charge prices related to market policy.

In principle, every Dutch family has its own family doctor. Only in exceptional circumstances (replacement) are general practitioner services sought elsewhere than from this family doctor. Ziekenfonds patients are bound by a formal regulation to make use, under normal circumstances, of the services of the family doctor on whose panel they are registered. A pregnant woman who wishes to be delivered by someone other than her own family doctor (perhaps because he is opposed to domiciliary maternity services) will meet with difficulties of a formal nature. Notwithstanding the possibility of choosing another family doctor (a possibility which frequently does not exist in rural districts) the patient is to a certain extent 'tied' as it were, to her own family doctor. There is a considerable amount of consumer attachment and this, too, constitutes a monopolistic aspect.

Another monopolistic aspect is evident in the situation relating to ziekenfons-insured women and midwives. If a midwife in a certain district comes to an arrangement with the ziekenfonds, the women who are insured with the ziekenfonds are, in principle, committed to employ the services of that midwife if they wish to claim reimbursement. The monopolistic character is strengthened by a large degree of heterogenity. This might be based on actual objective differences (e.g. better operating facilities in hospital than in the home) but it might also be founded on imagined differences. It is important to know to what extent preferences are based on valuation of real differences between the various services or on either imagined differences or insufficient knowledge. In a market where the suppliers are aiming at profit, advertisement fulfills an important function in giving the product an identity. Advertisement furthers the heterogenity of the product (or at least, the impression that consumers have of it) and consequently, also its monopolistic character. In the market for maternity services, the suppliers are able, in their advisory capacity, to emphasize its heterogenity and by doing so, to strengthen its monopolistic character.

There is a remarkable paradox between the ziekenfonds-insured and the privately-insured with regard to the price of services. Several of the monopolistic elements that the ziekenfonds-insured meet with on the supply side are the outcome of agreements reached between associations of suppliers and the ziekenfonds. This can be seen as an example of bilateral (collective) monopoly. This system of agreements in respect of ziekenfonds-insured patients makes it possible to keep a rein on the price of services while on the other hand, the privately-insured, who have in principle far more freedom of choice in the matter of maternity services, are confronted with prices which can be determined by the supplier to a much greater extent.

This examination of the market type can be summed up as follows. In

90

the quantitive sense there is a situation of few buyers and few sellers (combination of oligopoly-oligopsony). The individual purchaser is confronted with prices over which he, as participant in the market, can exercise practically no influence (polyopsony element) whilst there are clear monopoly elements present on the supply side.

Distinction can be made between prices in situations of perfect competition, which are subject to the workings of price mechanism, and controlled or administered prices. These latter are unilaterally determined by the suppliers (as, for example, fees charged by family doctors and specialists to privately-insured patients) or they are the outcome of negotiations between the participants in the market. As has been previously stated, the prices with which the ziekenfonds-insured are concerned are administered prices which have been agreed upon at the conference table. Analogous with the way in which the minimum wage is determined in the framework of collective bargaining in the labour market, so there can be said to be a 'pseudo-market' for materny services.

The fact that the turnover of maternity services is, to a certain extent, guaranteed regardless of price, is favourable to continuity of the production unit. There is a large degree of constancy in the turnover and there is relatively little danger of the commodity pricing itself out of the market. Some kind of countervailing action is, therefore, necessary in order to prevent waste as far as is possible. In the same way as the collective action of ziekenfonds organizations has this effect in respect of fees paid to family doctors, midwives and specialists (for ziekenfonds patients), the Central Office for Hospital Tariffs does the same thing for the price of hospital services.

In cases of medical indication, price has practically no effect on the demand for maternity services. In these cases, the price is seldom relevant for an individual consumer, whose individual risks are covered by insurance (ziekenfonds or private insurance). Participation of many means that purchasing power becomes concentrated and that, therefore, necessary purchase of a service is not hampered by financial considerations.

The doctors have at their disposal a powerful means of manipulation since it is they who diagnose medical indication. They are interested parties in the market process. The countervailing power of ziekenfonds

91

and insurances can exert but little restrictive influence on the determination of administered price.

The doctor engaged by the ziekenfonds to advise (control) has, too, only slight influence. All this puts a great strain on the motivations of those who supply the services, particularly of the doctors who play so important a part in determining the pattern of behaviour in this sector of the social system. The interests of the consumer have to be protected here by the ethical standards of the profession. There are in fact, three sets of interests at stake which may conflict one with another, namely the interests of the doctor himself, those of the consumer and those of society as a whole.

There is, in principle, a contradiction between the interests of one single insured person and those of society as a whole whenever the existence or absence of medical indication for hospitalization is in dispute. The insured person has individually much to gain financially if medical indication is diagnosed. His gain is paid, however from collectively-contributed premiums.

The doctor is confronted with this conflict of interests. If the diagnosis of medical indication permitted of no margin of uncertainty, the problem would be fairly simple. However, medical risk cannot be assessed in a mathematical way and it would, in many cases, be reasonable to defend either a positive or a negative decision as to the existence or absence of medical indication.

Professional jurisdiction and medical audit afford the means for the professional organizations to exercise their influence on the quality of the services supplied. Medical audit in particular, is still in a stage of development. Professional jurisdiction provides opportunities to adjust incorrect price determination especially in individual cases.

In the Dutch system of health services, the Government occupies an important place along with private organizations. The regulative powers of the Government are defined in various laws affecting the market for maternity services such as: the Law of Medical Practice, including regulations concerning obstetrical practice; the Ziekenfonds Law which defines the rights of insured persons; the Law on Hospital Tariffs which lays down the rules for determining the price of hospital services; the Law governing Hospital Accommodations and Facilities which includes amongst other things, regulations for the extention and adaptation of hospital services.

The supervisory task of the Government enables them to exert influence on the quality of the services. It concerns, for instance, recognition of hospitals and maternity homes, conditions to be fulfilled in order to obtain recognition, and control as to whether the conditions are indeed, fulfilled, as well as the laying down of training requirements and recognition of diplomas (midwives, maternity aids, doctors and (indirectly) specialists).

Governmental regulative powers affecting supply and demand also play a part in questions of subsidies. By means of subsidies it is possible to regulate the supply of services (the former bureaux for antenatal care, training of maternity aids) and to exercise influence on the price (subsidies for management of maternity centres, withdrawal of subsidies for salaries of maternity aids).

Financial support by the Government of research and experiment in the field of maternity services (obstetrical centres) should be regarded as a form of product development. Sometimes the Government itself takes on the onus of supplying services (Government hospitals).

Bibliography

Abel Smith, B., *An international study of health expenditure and its relevance for health planning*, W.H.O. Geneva, 1967.
–, Paying for health services, W.H.O. Geneva, 1963.
Albinsky, M., *Survey-research; een methode van sociaal wetenschappelijk onderzoek*, Utrecht, 1967.
Andriessen, J., *De ontwikkeling van de moderne prijstheorie*, 1955.
Ashford J. and Freyer J., Perinatal mortality, birth-weight, and place of confinement in England and Wales 1956-1965, In: *In the beginning; Studies of maternity services*, 1970.
Association for improvements in the maternity services, More midwives, London 1967.

Baay, J., *Een evaluatie van de poliklinische partus*, Cursus Ziekenhuisbeleid 1969/1970, Tilburg.
Baird, D., An area maternity service, *The Lancet*, March 1969, p. 515.
Barr, A., Classification of maternity hospitals on the basis of case cost, *The Hospital*, 1969/12.
Bergsma, J., Het klimaat maatgevend; *I.P.Z.*, jrg. 18 no. 12, 1970.
Blalock, H., *Social Statistics*, 1960.
Bout, J., *Moedersterfte in Nederland*, pfst, Leiden, 1971.
Brown, F., Evolution of a standard maternity unit, *Supplement to Hospital Management*, Nov./Dec., 1969.
Bridgman, R., *System of medical care*. In: *The theory and practice of public health*, London, 1969, pag. 430.
–, *The Rural Hospital, Its structure and organization*, W.H.O. Geneva, 1955.
Brotherston, J. and Forwell, G., Planning health services and the health team. In: *The theory and practice of public health*, London, 1969.
Bruyel, L., *Ziekenhuisopname en maatschappelijke omstandigheden*, Assen, 1958.
Buma, J., *Beschouwingen over de plaats van de huisarts in de Nederlandse gezondheidszorg*, N.I.P.G., Leiden, 1959.

Cavenagh, A., Place of Delivery: Dutch solution, *British medical Journal*, 15 June 1968.
Central Statistical Office, *Social trends*, London 1970, no. 1.
Centraal Bureau voor de Statistiek, *Statistisch Zakboek 1971*, 's-Gravenhage.
Chase, H., Perinatal and infant mortality in the United States and six West European countries. *American Journal of Public Health 57*: 1735, 1967.

94

Clark, A. e.a., *Patient Studies in maternal and child nursing*, Philadelphia, 1966.
Coe, R., *Sociology of medicine*, New York, 1970.
Consumentenbond, Ziektekostenverzekering, *Consumentengids*, Den Haag, augustus 1971.
–, Kraamtarieven, *Consumentengids*, juli 1968.
Cookson, I., The past and future of maternity service, *Journal of the College of General Practitioners*, 1967.13.143, March 1967.
Croxford, E., Focus on the maternity services, Recommendations by professional bodies – Present trends. *Nursing Times*, 13 Sept. 1968 (Occasional papers).

The Dan Mason nursing research committee of the National Florence NightingaleMemorial Committee, *Some aspects of the work of the midwive*, 1963.
Delfgaauw, G., *Inleiding tot de economische wetenschap, Theorie van het proces der prijsvorming*, Den Haag, 1965.
Department of health and social security, *National Health Service reorganisation. Consultative document*, May 1971, London.
–, *Confidential enquiry into post and neonatal deaths 1964-1966*, London, 1970.
–, *Central Health Services Council, Domiciliary midwifery and maternity bed needs*, London, 1970.
–, *Digest of health statistics for England and Wales*, London, 1969.
–, *Report on confidential enquires into maternal deaths in England and Wales 1964-1966* (idem 1961-1963 en 1958-1960), London, 1969.
Dolman, D., *Subsidies en gezondheidszorg. Een feitelijk onderzoek naar financieringsstructuren*, Leiden, 1964.
Drogendijk, A., Perinatale sterfte en verloskundige voorziening, *Ziekenfondsgids*, jrg. 18 no. 1 en 2, 1964.

Edwards, J., Needed: patient oriented nursing in the maternity unit, *Hospital Topics*, March 1970, p. 83.
Elderen, E. van – Van der Meer, Samenwerking huisarts-vroedvrouw. *Tijdschrift voor Sociale Geneeskunde*, jrg. 45 no. 10, 1967.
Entwistle, E., General view of the state of the midwifery profession today, In: *Family health care*, Conference, London, 1967.
Es, J. van, De toekomst van de huisarts in Nederland, *Huisarts en Wetenschap*, 6, 277, 1963.
–, en Pijlman, H., Het verwijzen van ziekenfondspatienten in 122 Nederlandse praktijken, *Huisarts en Wetenschap*, 13, 433.
Eskes, T. (1967), *Toekomstperspektief voor de verloskunde in Nederland*, Inleiding Nederlandse Gynaecologenvergadering, gehouden op 10 juni 1967.

Feldstein, M., *Economic analysis for health service efficiency*, Amsterdam, 1967.
Fokkens, O., Opnamecoëfficiënt en morbiditeitspatroon, *Ons Ziekenhuis*, no. 10, 1969.
Fry, J., G.P.-Obstetrics – has it a future? *International Medical Tribune of Great Britain*, May 12, 1966.
Functioneel overlegorgaan Volksgezondheid Enschede, *Rapport Kraamzorg Enschede, Problemen betreffende de verloskunde nu en in de toekomst in Enschede*, 1968.

95

Galloway, J., Domiciliary midwifery in Wolverhampton. *The Lancet. Public Health,* Oct. 26, 1968.

Gemeenschappelijk Overleg van Ziekenfondsorganisaties, *Documentatie,* april 1971.

Geneeskundige hoofdinspektie van de Volksgezondheid Leidschendam, Overzicht van de gehouden patiëntentelling op 23 april 1969 in de ziekenhuizen in Nederland (Leidschendam), 1970 (Idem tellingen 1964 en 1969).

–, *Jaarverslag 1969 van de Geneeskundig Hoofdinspekteur van de Volksgezondheid,* 1970 (Idem verslagen 1968 en 1967).

Geneeskundige Hoofdinspektie van de Volksgezondheid, *Rapport over de positie van de vroedvrouwen in Nederland,* 's-Gravenhage, 1963, no. 10/11.

–, *De kleine vroedvrouwen praktijken. Een onderzoek naar de omstandigheden van de vroedvrouwen met een praktijk van minder dan 75 bevallingen per jaar,* 's-Gravenhage, 1965, nr. 6.

–, *Overzicht van de gegevens van de ziekenhuizen in Nederland over het jaar 1968,* 1970 (Idem overzichten 1967 en 1968).

–, *Kraamzorg verleend in 1970,* 1971.

Geneeskundig Inspekteur van de Volksgezondheid voor Overijssel, *Nota verloskundige zorg Enschede,* 1969.

Goodman, N., *Alternatives to hospital care,* Strasbourg, 1963.

Groot, L., *Prijsvorming van ziekenhuisdiensten,* Roermond, 1960.

Gordon, I and Elias Jones T., The place of confinement: home or hospital? The mother's preference, *British Medical Journal,* 1,52, 1960.

Haas, J. de – Postuma, *Perinatale sterfte in Nederland, Onderzoek naar faktoren, die de perinatale sterfte beïnvloeden,* Assen, 1962.

–, Future trends in Maternal and Child Health, *Acta Paediatrica,* 47: 446-464, 1958.

–, *Perinatal mortality and maternity home helps in the Netherlands,* The International Children's Centre, Vol. III no. 2, 1954.

Haire, D. and Haire, J., Implementing family centered maternity care with a central nursery, *The International Childbirth Education Association,* Washington, 1971.

Hartgerink, M., Moederschapszorg en jeugdgezondheidszorg, In: *Sociale Geneeskunde,* redactie R. van Zonneveld, Amsterdam/Utrecht, 1968.

Hartog, F., *Hoofdlijnen van de prijstheorie,* Leiden, 1968.

Hofvander, Y., The health of mother and infant, In: *The theory and practice of public health,* London, 1969.

The Hospital centre for London, *Health visitors, district nurses and midwives working together in general practitioner service,* 1969.

Hospital Review and planning council of Southern New York, *Guidelines and recommendations for the planning and use of obstetrical facilities in Southern New York,* New York, 1966.

Huisjes, H., *Over doel, middel en maatstaf in de perinatale geneeskunde,* Groningen, 1971.

Huygen, F., De toekomst van de huisarts in Nederland (I, II), *Huisarts en Wetenschap,* 6.314, 6.347.

Janssen, M., *Zwangere en kraamvrouw in psychologisch perspektief,* Nijmegen/Utrecht, 1970.

Joint Committee of the Royal College of Obstetricians and Gynaecologists, *Maternity in Great Britain*, 1948.
De Jong, F., *Het systeem van de marktvormen*, Leiden, 1951.
De Jong, L., *Ziekenhuiskosten en ziekenhuistarief*, Amsterdam, 1967.
Jonge, H. de, *Inleiding tot de medische statistiek*, Deel I (N.I.P.G. Leiden), 1958.

King's Fund Hospital centre and The British Hospital Export Council (Diverse auteurs), Modern British maternity hospitals, *Supplement to Hospital Management*, Nov./Dec. 1969, Vol. 32, no. 397.
Kloosterman, G., De organisatievorm van de Nederlandse verloskunde en de verantwoordelijkheid daarbij van de Nederlandse gynaecologen, *Inleiding Nederlandse Gynaecologenvergadering*, gehouden op 10.6.1967.
–, De bevalling aan huis en de hedendaagse verloskunde, *Nederlands Tijdschrift voor de Geneeskunde*, 110, nr. 41, 1966.
–, Wording en bestaansreden van het consultatiebureau voor prenatale zorg, *Tijdschrift voor Sociale Geneeskunde*, 37, blz. 281, 1959.
Kweekschool voor Vroedvrouwen, *Veertig jaar R.K. Vereniging Moederschapszorg*, Heerlen, 1953.

Larsen, E., Terminal Rooming-in, *The American Journal of nursing*, Nov. 1956, Vol. 56 no. 11.
Leading Article, Changing Maternity services, *British medical Journal*, 23 Nov. 1968.
Leeuwe, J. de, Zwangeren, barenden, jonge moeders, *Nederlands Tijdschrift voor de Psychologie en haar grensgebieden*, 1966.

Maeck, J., Obstetrician – Midwife partnership in obstetric care, *Journal of Obstetrics and Gynaecology*, Febr. 1971.
Mannaerts, J., Rumoer rond het kraambed, *Ziekenfondsvragen*, jrg. XIV, 241.
Members of The Bradford Group of the College of General Practitioners, A survey of 100 early-discharge cases, *The lancet*, 1966, March 5, Special article.
Ministerie van Sociale Zaken en Volksgezondheid, *Volksgezondheidsnota*, 's-Gravenhage, 1966.

Nationale Federatie 'het Wit-Gele Kruis', *Funktie en struktuur van het Wit-Gele Kruis*, Utrecht, 1968.
–, *Jaarverslagen*, Utrecht, 1966/1970.
Nederlands Instituut voor Preventieve Geneeskunde, *Nota kraamzorg en hospitalisatie*, Leiden, 1965.
Nederlandse Huisartsen Genootschap (Werkgroep verloskunde van de huisarts), Verschillen in verloskundig handelen van huisartsen, *Huisarts en Wetenschap*, 9. 341, 1966.
–, Geboorten buiten de aanwezigheid van de arts, *Huisarts en Wetenschap*, 9. 310, 1966.
–, Enkele opmerkingen over prenatale zorg. Het eerste bezoek aan de huisarts, *Huisarts en Wetenschap*, 6. 75, 1963.
–, Kraamvrouwen naar maatschappelijke groepering, *Huisarts en Wetenschap*, 5. 10, 1962.

O'Brien, P., The general-practitioner obstetrician, *Lancet*, 2, 568.
Das öffentliche Gesundheitswesen, *Schwangern- und Säuglingsfürsorge in Frankreich*, Stuttgart, 1969.
Oostveen, C., De plaats van de vroedvrouw in de Nederlandse Gezondheidszorg, *Skriptie Cursus Ziekenhuisbeleid*, Tilburg, 1971.
Oxford Regional Hospital Board, *Safer obstetric care*, Oxford, 1967.

Peel, J., The Future of the maternity services, *Nursing Mirror*, 8 Nov., 1968.
Pel, A. en Pel-Mellink, J., Een duizendtal bevallingen in een huisartsenpraktijk, *Huisarts en Wetenschap*, 5. 133, 1962.
Provinciale Raad voor de Volksgezondheid in Zeeland, Kraamzorg in Zeeland, *Rapport over de gevolgen van de per 1 juni 1966 ingevoerde nieuwe financieringsregeling voor de kraamzorg*, 1967.
Pulles, P., Kraamzorg 'at risk', *Katholieke Gezondheidszorg*, 1970, pag. 413.

Richards, I., Donald, E. and Hamilton, F., Use of maternity care in Glasgow. In: *In the beginning; studies of maternity services*, 1970.
Ringholtz, S. and Morris, M., A test of some assumptions about rooming-in, *Nursing research*, 1961, Vol. 10, no. 4.
Robertson, J. and Carr, G., Late bookers for antenatal care. In: *In the beginning; Studies of maternity services*, 1970.
Rosengren, W. R., Some social psychological aspects of deliveryroom difficulties, *J. Nerv. ment. Dis.*, 132. 515, 1961.
Rottinghuis, H., Verloskunde nu en in de toekomst, *Ons Ziekenhuis*, maart, 1968.
The Royal College of Midwives, *Statements of policy on the maternity service*, London, 1968.
Royal College of obstetricians and gynaecologists, *The training of obstetricians and gynaecologists in Britain, and matters related thereto*, 1967.
Rubenstein, A., Massachusetts proposes maternity centers, *Modern Hospital*, July, 1968.
Russel, J. and Miller, M., Family responses to early discharge. In: *In the beginning; Studies of maternity services*, 1970.

Sande, W. van der, De samenwerking van een huisarts met een vroedvrouw, *Huisarts en Wetenschap*, 9. 265, 1966.
Santema, S. en Dahler, A., Enkele demografische en financiële beschouwingen over de georganiseerde interne kraamzorg in de provincie Utrecht, *Tijdschrift voor de Sociale Geneeskunde*, jrg. 41 no. 11, 1963.
Schweisheimer, W., Her baby by her side, Rooming-in in the U.S.A., *Nursing Times*, Dec. 19, 1958.
Schmidt, A., *De toekomst van de obstetricus*, 1968.
Seelen, J., Vrezen rondom de nataliteit, *Katholieke Gezondheidszorg*, jrg. 38. 8, 1969.
Sikkel, A., *Optimale verloskunde*, Leiden, 1966.
Smulders, A., Verloskundige hulp in 4 huisartsenpraktijken uit de vorige eeuw, *Huisarts en Wetenschap*, 5. 290, 1962.
Spicer, G. and Lipworth, L., Regional and social factors in infant mortality, *Studies on medical and population subjects*, nr. 19, 1966.

Stallworthy, J., Changes in midwifery – progression or regression? *Nursing Mirror*, Febr. 7, 1969.

Stearn, R. and Fisher, J., The place of domiciliary midwifery – The Obstetrician, The General practitioner *Midwives Chronicle & Nursing notes*, November 1968.

Stichting Centraal Orgaan Ziekenhuistarieven, *Jaarverslagen 1967/1968/1969/1970*, Utrecht.

Stolte, J., *Naar optimale vormen*, Nijmegen, 1966.

–, *Vraag naar en aanbod van gezondheidszorg en ziekenhuisdiensten*, Tilburg, 1965.

Swaak, A., Naar een optimale verloskundige hulp, *Medisch Contact*, 1970/47.

–, Medische en funktionele aspekten van de kraamzorg, *Tijdschrift voor de Sociale Geneeskunde*, 46e jrg. no. 20, oktober 1968.

–, De invloed van verbetering van de arbeidsvoorwaarden op het ziekteverzuim bij kraamverzorgsters, *Tijdschrift voor de Sociale Geneeskunde*, 44, 1966, 473.

Theobald, G., Home on the second day; the Bradford experiment, *British Medical Journal*, 2, 1364, 1959.

Thompson, J. and Fetter, R., The economics of the maternity services, The Yale, *Journal of Biology and Medicine*, Vol. 36, no. 1, August 1963.

Thompson, J. e.a., Use of computer simulation techniques in predicting requirements for maternity facilities, *Hospitals*, Febr. 1963.

Topliss, E., Selection procedure for hospital and domiciliary confinements. In: *In the beginning; Studies of maternity services*, 1970.

Tulder, J., *De beroepsmobiliteit in Nederland van 1919 tot 1954*, Leiden, 1962.

United States Department of Health, Education and Welfare, *Planning the labor-delivery Unit in the General hospital*, Washington, 1964.

–, *Maternity care utilization and financing*, Washington, 1964.

University of Michigan, *The economics of health and medical care*.

Verboom, A., *Verloskunde in een huisartsenpraktijk*, Haarlem, 1968.

Verbrugge, H., *Kraamzorg bij thuisbevallingen*, Groningen, 1968.

–, Interne kraamzorg, *Tijdschrift voor de Sociale Geneeskunde*, jrg. 43 no. 9, 30 april 1964.

Viegas, C., Advantages of the rooming-in plan for mother and baby, *I.P.H. Hospital de Hoje*, Vol. 21, Ano IX, 1964.

Vromen, M., Bevalling thuis of in de kliniek, *Ziekenfondsgids*, jrg. 19 no. 3, 1965.

Williams, B., 48-hour maternity discharge – good or bad?, *Nursing Mirror*, Oct. 11, 1968.

Ziekenfondsraad, *Verslagen van de Ziekenfondsraad over de jaren 1965/1969*, Amsterdam.

Zuidijk, J., Is de kraamzorg werkelijk zo duur?, *Ziekenfondsgids*, jrg. 21 (1967, no. 7/8).